D0722166

MALLARMÉ: *IGITUR*

Mallarmé Igitur

ROBERT GREER COHN

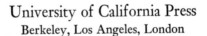

University of California Press
Berkeley, Los Angeles, London

University of California Press
Berkeley and Los Angeles, California
University of California Press, Ltd.
London, England
© 1981 by
The Regents of
the University of California

Printed in
the United States of America

1   2   3   4   5   6   7   8   9

Library of Congress Cataloging in Publication Data
Cohn, Robert Greer
    Mallarmé: Igitur.
    Includes the text of Igitur.
    Bibliography: p.
    1.   Mallarmé, Stéphane, 1842–1898.   Igitur.
I.   Mallarmé, Stéphane, 1842–1898.   Igitur.   1981.
II.   Title.
PQ2344.I43C6   848'.807   80–24613
ISBN 0–520–04188–7

for Norma
"cette soeur sensée et tendre"

Contents

Abbreviations

Corr.	*Stéphane Mallarmé: Correspondance, 1862–1871.* Edited by Henri Mondor. Gallimard, 1959.
O.	Robert Greer Cohn. *L'Oeuvre de Mallarmé: Un Coup de Dés.* Librairie Les Lettres, 1951.
T.P.	Robert Greer Cohn. *Toward the Poems of Mallarmé.* University of California Press, 1966.
N.	Gardner Davies, ed. *Les Noces d'Hérodiade: Mystère.* Gallimard, 1959.
T.	*Touches* (the second part of the text of *Igitur*, variants mostly).
Page	The capitalized word indicates the double-page of the *Coup de Dés*.

Page numbers without other reference are to the *Oeuvres complètes*, Gallimard, 1945.

Preface

Igitur was first published posthumously by Mallarmé's son-in-law, Dr. Edmond Bonniot, at Gallimard in 1925. The present study follows the later publication in the Pléiade edition of the *Oeuvres complètes* (Gallimard, 1945). All numbers without other indication are to the pages of this edition.

I had originally planned to consult the MS of *Igitur* in the hands of a private collector in Paris, or at least copies that a few individuals had made. But the poet and critic, Yves Bonnefoy, who is well-informed on Mallarméana, assures me that there are no important variants in the MS and that the version printed by Bonniot, and duplicated by Mondor in the Pléiade edition and in Bonnefoy's own edition at Gallimard in 1976, is entirely sufficient for our purposes here.

There is one fragment published by Henri Charpentier, in the special number of *Les Lettres* of 1948 devoted to Mallarmé, which I have included in the text at the indicated juncture.

After two tentative introductory passages (*Ancienne Étude* and *4 Morceaux*), Mallarmé's sketchy text is made up of five main sections, each identified by a roman numeral. The rest is variant passages called *Touches* (or *Scolies*), which I identify by the letter *T.* followed by the roman numeral that corresponds to the main section; thus *T*.II is the variant passage "retouching" section II.

In "Text and Detailed Commentary" I have broken up the text into manageable portions—usually paragraphs—numbered consecutively from A to Z (+ AA, AB, AC, AD).

A comment on previous studies will be found in the appendix.

A generous grant from the National Endowment for the Humanities made this study possible. I am extremely grateful to the Endowment and to Editions Gallimard for permission to print, in successive fragments with commentary, the text of *Igitur* as it appears in the *Oeuvres complètes* of Mallarmé, Bibliothèque de la Pléiade, 1945. To Henri Peyre and to my wife Valentina, too, my abiding thanks.

I am indebted to Georges Poulet for encouraging this project with an enthusiastic comment on the Appendix devoted to *Igitur* in my *Oeuvre de Mallarmé: Un Coup de Dés*: "Vous m'avez expliqué *Igitur*." A few words like that from a master like Poulet can go a long way. The support of William J. McClung at the University of California Press was enormously helpful and is warmly appreciated. Peter Gibian deserves appreciative mention for being an attentive reader of my manuscript.

Portions of the book previously appeared in *Romanic Review* (no. 60, 1969), *L'Oeuvre de Mallarmé: Un Coup de Dés* (Librairie Les Lettres, 1951), and *Modes of Art* (Anma Libri, 1975). I am beholden to the editors and publishers for permission to reprint.

I

Introduction

1. Preliminaries

IN THE MONTH of August 1870, in sunny Avignon, Catulle Mendès and Villiers de l'Isle-Adam stopped by, on their way back from a Wagnerian pilgrimage, to see their friend and literary companion in arms, Stéphane Mallarmé. He was delighted to see them and eager to read them his latest work, *Igitur ou la folie d'Elbehnon*, an exceedingly mysterious and austere metaphysical story. Mendès, despite his fondness for Mallarmé, was puzzled and rather irritated at Villiers for approving what seemed to him an unfathomable and aberrant text. His irritation may have had some point: one doubts that Villiers really understood the text, which in some respects has resisted exegetes, including the most expert Mallarmistes, ever since. Still, the metaphysical story or play was familiar territory to Villiers—witness his own *Isis* and *Axël*—and he no doubt intuitively grasped some of the somber beauty going on deep underground in that hauntingly self-probing, starkly intense prose.

What impression can he have caught in that first challenging exposure? A vision of an implacably daring and stubborn explorer of the unknown like himself, with echoes of Hamlet and of an immemorial occult tradition of initiation into life's rock-bottom mysteries, going back to ancient lore like the Upanishads, the Greek and early Christian mystics, and the Hebrew Kabbalah and rising in time to modern figures like Swedenborg, Böhme, Poe, Balzac, and Nerval. In sum, the core of *Igitur* is a spiritual adventure described by, among others, Carl Jung in *Psyche and Symbol* and Joseph Campbell in his *Hero with a Thousand Faces*: a descent into the dark womb of the unconscious, eternal night, and reemergence, rebirth to a vision of undying light and truth. The hero strips himself of earthly clutter, becomes as naked as a babe. It is a sacrificial, bitter experience, involving a psychic suicide, a baptismal plunge into unbreathable depths of the self and the cosmos.

In this initiatory moment, at a dark Midnight in a claustral room with drawn curtains where space as well as time is annulled in a diamond-point of ultimate consciousness, the solitary spirit communes with his dead ancestors, who have handed him down a mysterious mandate in a magic book, illuminated by a single candle that at the fateful instant he will blow out, leaving only a deathly blackness and void. Then the hero will throw the dice of universal chance, accepting its absurdity as he does death-anguish, in order to find true Meaning and Life.

There are further episodes, such as the exit from the room and descent into a stairway of the inner self, down to the tomb of the past. All this Villiers could have followed at least in essential outline.

Villiers may have overheard too the echoes of Shakespeare's Macbeth: "Out, out, brief candle! / Life's but . . . a poor player / That struts and frets his hour upon the stage. . . . a tale / Told by an idiot, full of sound and fury, / Signifying nothing." When Villiers died, Mallarmé referred to him as a "histrion véridique," unquestionably recalling the passage from *Macbeth* and, even more powerfully, the ontological drama of the absurd—"to be or not to be"—played out for all time by that ambiguously mad, clowning, suicidally tragic figure, Hamlet.

Igitur, as we see it now, after Claudel and many another commentator, is a sort of nakedly epistemological and ontological Hamlet story. It represents a truth proclaimed by Baudelaire in "Le Peintre de la vie moderne": that genius is childhood prolonged or regained. Whether, with its naive purity and emotional power, that childhood is "retrouvée à volonté" is something Proust would want to dispute, but in any case it comes back through a grid of mature tempering, the rationally normative, "horizontal" dimension of the spirit—which today we are apt to identify with Jakobson's "metonymy." This coolness is characteristic of *Igitur* as well: the Poe-inspired mood of hyperlucidity and control.

The fundamental tension of existential struggle, "to be or not to be," which every child on the threshold of this world must feel as it emerges from the All or the maternal womb—and, later, their avatars[1]—is certainly aggravated in genius. Genius hesitates at every stage, addicted as it is to the depths and heights of its key question, "hung up" on the problem of evil or "What's it all about?" It has trouble going on, particularly at the crucial crossroads between childhood and maturity, when the problem can be put as "to become or not to become."

1. The basic problem is the absurd—"la fiction ... le procédé même de l'esprit" (*Notes*, p. 851)—which arises again in the "mirror stage" and the Oedipal stage of total attraction and refusal; also in language, which, contrary to Noam Chomsky, is always *both* above (free) and below (innate).

Such is Mallarmé's vision of Hamlet, our "juvenile shadow" or "adolescent vanished from us" with his "difficulty in becoming"—likewise his vision of Hérodiade, Hamlet's female cousin, as it were. She, a singularly self-sufficient princess, poetically representing Mallarmé's anima, struggles mightily—like other highly "individuated" or headstrong girls—before yielding to fate via the agency of the male (the animus, represented by the divine piercing look of St. Jean), eventually accepting his intervention for the sake of the splits in Being that are the essence of Becoming, and thus changing into a new version of herself, a wife and mother, a mature woman, a queen.[2]

This drama, of course, reflects the parallel maturation of the artist, who goes not at all gently into that psychic death, or sense of Nothing—the *gouffre* of Pascal and Baudelaire, the *néant* of Proust—the hollow male womb whence a superior artistic birth will spring. As Baudelaire says of Manet, "the artist cries with terror before being overcome" by Creation, the source of his creation (*Le Confiteor de l'artiste*). God here, in these rare unmediated instances, plays the role of the male agent, possessing the artist "from behind"—as Sartre puts it in *La Nausée*, nausea being a sort of creative morning sickness preceding a birth, that of his art. This drama of maturation is the substance of Mallarmé's correspondence and of his production in the 1860s (his age: 18–28), i.e., the period of his late adolescence, which is

2. At least *en puissance*, as hinted at in various fragments. The splits range from epistemologico-metaphysical unity become duality to such physical equivalents as the parting of the labia, the biological initial division of the ovum, and so on. The reluctance to "die to live" (*mourir et devenir*) or to accept the shocking invasion of sex and the male is perpetuated in the contemporary wave of anorexia in young girls.

generally prolonged in genius of this stripe. The crisis culminates in the figure of Hérodiade, in the mid-sixties, reflected by *Igitur*, a few years later; the story was halted, unfinished, in 1869.

Life is more beautiful and terrifying—Mallarmé's "hilarité et horreur" (*Coup de Dés*)—than most humans like to think as they busily go about breaking up its violent forces; but artists, more idle, vulnerable, and honest, are apt to experience its infinites more purely. The ambivalence of great and "serious" art with its powerful ordeals of pain is a homeopathic way of dealing with the unbearable assaults of reality, both for the artist and, more vicariously or mediatedly, for his public. At times, as in every adventure, the power of the negative is almost too much for the creator. Mallarmé's doubt—or self-doubt—was almost prohibitive, taking the form of an asymptotically approached perfectionism and reserve that at times threatened total sterility. It is one of his obsessive themes. Fortunately, as we know, the positive poles—artistic triumph, vertically; horizontally, his on-going ("feminine") health—won out, but it often seems nip and tuck, as we follow his correspondence, as if he wouldn't make it.

The rhythmic series of convulsive ups and downs, like that in labor of parturition, leads to a final eruptive event, the overwhelming vision of a Great Work, which we follow in the splendid letters to Henri Cazalis and Théodore Aubanel.

J'ai rencontré deux abîmes, qui me désespèrent. L'un est le Néant. . . . Oui, *je le sais*, nous ne sommes que de vaines formes de la matière—mais bien sublimes pour avoir inventé Dieu et notre âme. Si sublimes, mon ami! que je veux me donner ce spectacle de la matière, ayant conscience d'être et cependant, s'élançant forcenément dans le rêve qu'elle sait n'être pas, chantant l'Ame et toutes les divines impressions pareilles qui se sont amassées en nous depuis les premiers âges, et proclamant devant le Rien qui est la vérité, ces glorieux mensonges! (to Cazalis, April 1866; *Corr.*, pp. 207–8)

The honest ambivalence of "the absurd" will remain the key tone of Mallarmé and his major lineage through existentialism, structuralism, and the like in the twentieth century. However, in Mallarmé the syntactical Vision that results from the experience of Nothing becomes a lacework of beauty, which, in contradistinction to Valéry and most of our moderns, he never abandons. He *believed* to that extent ("On ne peut se passer d'Eden"), and the *glorieux* of the *glorieux mensonges*, as in the Christian doctrine of the resurrected body— the *corps glorieux*—redeems, remotely and unsentimentally but way-way-out ultimately, the emptied modern eschatological scene of matter and of humans as mere matter. His vision will soon, in the letters, take on a tilt toward affirmation and the joy of art:

Je suis en train de jeter les fondements d'un livre sur le Beau, Mon esprit se meut dans l'Eternel, et en a eu plusieurs frissons, si l'on peut parler ainsi de l'Immuable [this illustrates well the artist's shift to presence, rhythms—of *frissons*—concrete existence]. Je me repose à l'aide de trois courts poèmes, mais qui seront inouïs, tous trois à la glorification de la Beauté. (to Cazalis, May 1866, *Corr.*, p. 216)

Or:

Après avoir trouvé le Néant, j'ai trouvé le Beau—et que tu ne peux t'imaginer dans quelles altitudes lucides je m'aventure. . . . *Hérodiade*, où je m'étais mis tout entier sans le savoir. . . . (to Cazalis, July 1866, *Corr.*, pp. 220–21)

And:

> Trois poèmes en vers, dont *Hérodiade* est l'Ouverture,
> mais d'une pureté que l'homme n'a pas atteinte. . . . Et
> quatre poèmes en prose, sur la conception spirituelle
> du néant. Il me faut dix ans: les aurai-je? (to Cazalis,
> May 1867, *Corr.*, p. 242)

No question: the Vision that was to haunt him over
a lifetime, with or without the midwifery of Hegel's influence (which I doubt was of decisive significance in
any event, even if he really read Hegel, which is dubious, too), was triumphantly born at this juncture. Like
the powerful force at the heart of a motor or atomic in-
stallation, the Vision had to be "jacketed," harnessed
into metonymic "put-puts," as it were, into rhythmic
production through work. He had to find the right combination of its aliveness and its control. At times the
Vision was buried into stagnancy, out of fear of its vi-
olence, as we read in *Prose (pour des Esseintes)*: "dans
un livre de fer vêtu." When he was up to it, the genie
would be gingerly taken again from the bottle, as he
tried out new forms for its expression. The precarious-
ness accounts, obviously, for the intermittence of its
apparition in his life.

When it was first born it was of course *too much* of
a good thing—the repeated *trop* of *Prose (pour des Esseintes)* and the letters. At first he wrote confidently:
"Tu vois j'imite la loi naturelle" (to Aubanel, 16 July
1866); then came a breakdown, and "la nature, elle est
trop [my italics] faussée en moi, et monstrueuse, pour
que je me laisse aller à ses voies" and "ma pensée, oc-
cupée par la plénitude de l'Univers et distendue perdait
sa fonction normale . . . le trop plein [note *trop*] de
[ma] pensée. . . ." (to Cazalis, 4 February 1869, p. 299).

This is just about the time he resorted to the curative powers of *Igitur*.

Later he would say to Ghil: "Ce n'est qu'à travers ... des ans d'étude et point dès l'éclair révélateur qu'on peut le [the Great Work] traiter définitivement" (*Les Dates et les Oeuvres*, Crès, 1923, p. 92). He had learned the famous *patience* that is the keynote of *Prose* (*pour des Esseintes*). But at first, after the initial explosion of "l'éclair révélateur," he was left as empty, or flooded by a black backwash, as many a new mother—some kill themselves, it is known—or a too-hopeful and bitterly disappointed lover, dreaming of a new self. One thinks, for example, of the image, arising in world literature four years later, of the burned-out bush, following Rimbaud's fever of composition in the *Saison en enfer*.[3]

When Mallarmé speaks of *le Néant*, it is pure Negation, total, perhaps located at a microcosmic zero core or macrocosmically in those empty *espaces infinis* imagined by Pascal (and later by Mallarmé in *Quand l'ombre menaça* or the *Coup de Dés*). The vertical dimension of that Negation is the deep blackness of "Shadow" in horror of psychic death—the *ombre* of *Quand l'ombre*, the *nue* of *A la nue*—"the dark night of the soul" (San Juan de la Cruz); its horizontal dimension is the flat "indifféremment le Hasard" of the *Coup de Dés*. That is perhaps worse, closer to the *Néant* (or the *Rien* of the *Coup de Dés*), but since the dimensions are dialectically related in polypolar epistemology—Mallarmé's, put in my own discursive terms—we need not quibble about it yet. In any event the horizontal dimension appears early and throughout Mallarmé's correspondence and work as the

3. Some comparison of *Une Saison en enfer* and *Igitur* will be found in my *The Poetry of Rimbaud*, Princeton University Press, 1973, pp. 406–407.

theme of *ennui*, *névrose*, and sterility or impotence. This
—either "dark" or "flat"—inability of the spirit to rise
in, or to, an act *vertically* (impotence) is prolonged
horizontally in time as *ennui*. These two interrelated dimensions meet microcosmically in a zero core of *Néant*,
which is dialectically related to its positive aspect, *l'Absolu*. Hence: "névrose, ennui (ou Absolu!)" (III, O).
The backwash from the Hérodiade-Vision took an aggravated form of the monster of *ennui*, prolonging the
sterility that, in the letter to Cazalis, he wants to exorcize
by writing a curative work (the theme, the drama of
exorcism, appears prominently in the text, as we shall
see). This is a version of the homeopathic self-therapy
that all art is first, releasing through expression—cathar-
tically—the "pity and terror" and, worse, nothingness,
that, second, one purges in others. So Mallarmé gave up
momentarily the notion of going on with the Great
Work, which he had been speaking of fervently to his
closest friends. On 14 November 1869 he wrote to Cazalis that he had spent part of his summer on a

> travail que je te porterai l'été prochain: c'est un conte
> par le quel [*sic*] je veux terrasser le vieux monstre de
> l'Impuissance, son sujet, du reste, afin de me cloîtrer
> dans mon grand labeur déjà réétudié. S'il est fait (le
> conte) je suis guéri; similia similibus. (*Corr.*, p. 313)

Two years previously, in the letter of May 1867 to
Cazalis cited above, he had described his future Work
as including "quatre poèmes en prose, sur la conception
spirituelle du néant." It is idle to speculate whether one
of those prose poems was the nucleus of *Igitur* since
almost everything is related in Mallarmé's thought and
work. The mood in which he describes the writing of
Igitur to Cazalis is rather different from that of the

known prose poems or poems in verse, but the starkest and darkest of them, such as *A la nue* or *Ses purs ongles* or *Quand l'ombre menaça*, clearly overlap in their central imagery and central drama with *Igitur*. But momentarily, at least, he saw *Igitur* not as part of the Great Work but as a means toward getting the appetite to tackle it. Something like that partial self-deception (as it were: "I'm not really writing, that crazy enterprise, but doing something that deals with it") characterized his correspondence about *Ses purs ongles*; in my commentary on that sonnet (in *T.P.*) I observed that, in spite of his claim that the poem had nothing to do with his Work, it does indeed reflect the latter's major themes, as does everything of importance he wrote.[4]

Rimbaud, on the point of uttering his *dernier couac*, wrote his *Saison en enfer* for similar desperate reasons, as I try to show in *The Poetry of Rimbaud*, i.e., to purge himself of a destructive excess of thought or poetic vision by its radical expression in a modified—more calculated, metonymically or systematically controlled, narrative even—guise. *Igitur* in this sense follows the example of Poe through a coldly deductive, detective deliberateness of style, which uses a civilized form of deadly precision, almost murderous in its "cool," to deal with a murderer or murderous principle in the cosmos. This is, broadly speaking, a classic dimension of art. Another seminal illustration of the switch, the delicate

4. This is a common maneuver of literati, e.g., "Ceci n'est pas un livre" penned at the head of a book like *La Vie de Marianne* or the familiar fiction "I found this MS in a trunk" (*Le Grand Meaulnes, La Nausée*). In these cases, however, it is a question of *pudeur* rather than of gingerliness. More typical of the latter are writers like Joyce and Mann who fool themselves into thinking they are writing short stories—which turn out to be *Ulysses* and *The Magic Mountain*!

self-preserving maneuver whose structure is parallel
to everyman's mutation to maturity, is the change of
Goethe's manner from the *Sturm und Drang* suicidal
Romanticism of *Werther* to the neoclassic willed seren-
ity of *Iphigenia*. But, fortunately for art, the trick suc-
ceeds only partially and not for long: the daemons of
resurgent romanticism—or the "daemonic dimension"—
come back manifold, as in the Gospels, within both the
curative document and the subsequent work of the in-
curable genius, who more or less learns just "to live
with" his malaise.

That is, if he is lucky: the homeopathic cure—as
Charles Saint-Évremond long ago worriedly observed
about catharsis—can kill. It helped to kill the poet in
Rimbaud, at least; in Mallarmé's case the remedy apparently worked. Mallarmé seems to have had it out with
himself, gone *jusqu'au bout* in this direction, at least for
a while. The death of his son Anatole in 1879 sparked
a return to the dangerous depths. There were other
plunges, and soarings, later, recorded partially in the
fragments called *Le Livre*, most fully in the *Coup de
Dés*.[5] But as we learn from the correspondence and the
known facts of his life in Paris in the seventies, Mallarmé
did return from pure epistemological exploration and
bare metaphysical drama to something more developed,
via dialectical interfusion with the median realm of reality, or presence—something more full, rounded, aesthetic. In the mid-eighties *Prose (pour des Esseintes)*
tells how he learned *patience*—the key word of the poem
—as a means to this end, from his tender and wise sis-
ter-soul, his anima—life-as-presence, *shekhina*, on-going
élan, and memory, with vestiges of actual girls or

5. See *Mallarmé's Masterwork: New Findings*, Part II.

women important to him.[6] And the Great Work, when a major sketch of it, at least, appeared, did profit in richness from its dialectical return to the "feminine" norm of life after his risky ascension and plunge, as in crucial episodes of the world's religious or mystic tradition.[7]

What helped him to give up this direction of mental excess was the elusive, homeopathically confronted nature of mind "chasing its own tail," the "infinite regress" that is the condition of its liberty and that a long line of thinkers from Plato and Aristotle to Camus has encountered.[8] Igitur seemed momentarily to have won a sort of victory by "losing all to gain all" in a psychic suicide recalling the Gospels, or Dostoevsky's Kirilov—"swallowing" meaninglessness, the absurd chance, like a poison and thus defeating the sentimental religious hope of his ancestors, their "maladie d'idéalité." But midway through the text there is a clear statement of the absurd itself having the last word—or at least always a further word—in attempts like this:

> Bref dans un acte où le hasard est en jeu, c'est toujours le hasard qui accomplit sa propre Idée en s'affirmant ou se niant. (p. 441)

Here, and in the rest of the passage, "chance" is also the absurd, i.e., a paradoxical whirl of chance-determinism, infinite-finite, and so on.

I think of the graffito: "God is dead [signed] Nietz-

6. See *T.P.*, pp. 244–45.

7. One thinks of Moses, Dionysian ritual, Jesus, St. Patrick, Zarathustra. . . . See Joseph Campbell, *A Hero with a Thousand Faces* (Pantheon Books, 1949).

8. The fact that when Mallarmé read *Igitur* in 1869 to Villiers and Catulle Mendès the latter stamped his foot in disapproval would not, I think, in itself cause the abandonment of the enterprise as some (e.g., Guy Michaud) have surmised.

sche," under which a naturally mysterious hand had written: "Nietzsche is dead [signed] God."

Hence the many critics who see *Igitur* as the germ of *Coup de Dés*, or as an important stage leading to it, are on the right track, but with the following reservations: greater emphasis should be put on the bare bones nature of *Igitur*, which, at least willfully—as a self-curative, quite abstract or reflexive attempt, rather than a full fling at Vision and its incarnation in art, beauty, poetic "flesh"—departs from the main route of the *Grand Oeuvre*, most fully represented by the *Coup de Dés*; second, the asymmetric victory of Being expressed in various tentative fragments has no equivalent in the later cosmogonic Poem, where all is supreme Game, evanescence, except for a glimmering glimpse of a wistful possibility . . .

But on the whole, since our text eventually abandons the attempt to fix reality in a finality—having encountered the "infinite regress" of the absurd and, as I will demonstrate here anew, a more sophisticated polypolar form of the absurd—in a way that the critics have scanted, *Igitur* turns out to be at least tentatively on the main route of Mallarméan epistemology. And some important items of imagery are left over in the later Work: the stripling Hamletlike figure becomes the *prince amer de l'écueil*, the *naufrage* of his ancestors in its metaphysical sense becomes a part of the major imagery; the *château* of Igitur, which is also the monument of his self-sacrificial act, turns into the *manoir* of the *Coup de Dés*, with a further note of impermanence; and the dice theme itself builds into the central thread of the masterpiece, though, again, with no final throw as opposed to the at least momentary notion of a *coup* pulled off in *Igitur*. But the scene moves from the claustral midnight

chamber to all outdoors,[9] a storm-wracked ocean as
the ground-bass line of imagery on which is superimposed the whole evolutionary drama of man's Becoming,
a cosmogony in outline (*portative*, as Raymond Queneau might say); this diachronic development is barely
sketched in *Igitur*—a few words about the *ancêtres* and
their ancient shipwreck, and so on. The expansion in
perspective in both space and time is enormous from
one work to the other.

The genesis of *Igitur* can be traced from Shakespeare's
Hamlet—which Mallarmé, after Hugo and Baudelaire,
saw as the drama of Man—through a series of modern
Hamlet figures: William Beckford, the author of *Vathek*, as Mallarmé portrays him in his preface to that
work; Poe, as we glimpse him from *The Raven* or *The
Fall of the House of Usher*; another aristocratic son of
late civilization, Villiers de l'Isle-Adam, to whom Mallarmé read the story; Baudelaire himself; and so on.

As in the case of the *Coup de Dés*, it seems sensible
to determine "what a thing is before explaining how it
got that way," so the main part of the genetic portion
of this study—i.e., works influencing Mallarmé, plus relatively remote echoes in his earlier work—is relegated
to the end of the volume where it can grow, as it could
endlessly, given the interpenetrating nature of all Mallarmé's writings, without getting in the way of the main
business of investigating the text itself.

By the same token, the line of development leading
from *Igitur* to the *Coup de Dés* will be left at this juncture in the sketchy form outlined above: it has been
explored in detail in my *L'Oeuvre de Mallarmé: Un
Coup de Dés* and throughout my *Mallarmé's Master-*

9. This was hinted at in the sea-sky foam and stars suggested
by the clock gleams.

work: New Findings, where much posthumously published material was added to the earlier perspective.

I believe that Mallarmé gave up on his early enterprise not only because of the endless dilemma that he, like every other profound thinker—and was there ever a profounder?—encountered deep down and in (or "far out," to speak macrocosmically), but also because of what he felt to be its comparative aesthetic sterility, its one-sided abstractness.[10] The story is fleshed out in a cluster of images that have poetic valences and echo through the rest of the *oeuvre* as well as with each other —this is largely an aspect of the total harmony ("vertically," "circularly," or "metaphorically") of the vision, which is vibrantly alive, artistic to that extent. But the images are rather stark and denotative, as geometrically crisp as the angular dice cubes, for example, which indeed add a modern and perhaps "cubist" understatement to the poetry, along the rational metonymic axis that is also the direction of the cool rationality of Poe. That bare quality, in combination with the humbly fragmentary, open, unfinished nature of the sketch, has given it a certain contemporary appeal, in line with the doctrine of Hugo Friedrich (*The Modern Lyric*), but which, I think, has little to do with the way Mallarmé saw it or, indeed, its true enduring worth.

What may appear as fragmentary in most of Mallarmé's production is really the effect of refinement and aeration: the organic and harmonious connection of the parts is so open and free—the constellatory phenomena of the *Jeu suprême*—because the links of ordinary reality

10. An immediate reason for giving up the project was that, despite its special nature, it too was dangerously excessive and exhausting. But that would not account for its being permanently left in abeyance . . .

in everyday existence and usual syntagmatic language are suppressed in favor of the aesthetic of *suggestion*; further, the underlying structure of deeper (philosophic, etc.) reality is itself hidden—as if wires or plumbing were concealed under carpets or in basement or attic—according to the Poe doctrine to which Mallarmé very consciously subscribed: "Je révère l'opinion de Poe, nul vestige d'une philosophie, l'éthique ou la métaphysique ne transparaîtra; j'ajoute qu'il la faut, incluse et latente" ("Sur Poe," p. 872).

Igitur's fragmentariness is either the result of its being unfinished, which has nothing to do with its intent, or of the airy, suggestive, phenomenological quality of Mallarmé's art and thought, which is harmonious underneath (the very Mallarméan word and concept *épars* is illustrative of this extreme union of opposites: a vast scattering, supported by the direct sense and the flat *a* —of *vaste, espace,* etc.—is offset, in an appropriate context, by the harmonizing intimate *ar* cluster with its tender *r*).[11] The unfinished aspect may feed the pure, clean appearance of the suggestive aspect, but that is inadvertent. In any event, one must distinguish between superficial effects, seized upon by modernists—Filippe Marinetti and Apollinaire, for example, who exploited the *Coup de Dés* in this way—and the full, rounded Symbolist reality of Mallarmé.

Nevertheless, Mallarmé's plunge into the structures of consciousness in order to radically rethink the world, as boldly as a Descartes, left, in this instance, effects at the surface of the text that are an important part of the modern aesthetic. One may say even that they *tran-*

11. Cf. the latest view of the neutrino: its motion (doing) stems from the Big Bang; its mass (being) can collectively collapse the cosmos.

spired through his later, fuller Work, certainly in the form of the dice image, along with the daring typography, as it appeared to Picasso, Braque, and Gris, who took that structural aspect of the poem and made it into something nakedly contemporary and visual.

In "Picasso's Musical and Mallarméan Construction," Ronald Johnson, writing in *Arts Magazine* (March 1977), demonstrates Picasso's indebtedness to the *Coup de Dés*, not only for the dice theme, but for a general open aesthetic. Kenneth Rexroth, in the preface to his translations of Pierre Reverdy (New Directions, 1969), extends this influence to cubism altogether, including Reverdy. Henri Peyre had previously mentioned that Picasso and Gris came to Paris largely because of Mallarmé (in *Connaissance de Baudelaire*, Corti, 1951, p. 152). As exciting as all this is, honesty dictates that we see these departures as representing only partially what Mallarmé's literary and inclusive art means for the ages.

In cognate fashion, I must register a certain distance from the perspective of the *Tel Quel* group as presented, for example, in the article "Une Lecture d'*Igitur*" by Pierre Rottenberg (*Tel Quel*, no. 3, 1967). For them, Mallarmé expresses a radically anti-idealistic temper—antibourgeois, generally deconstructive, materialist in that neo-Marxist sense. The *deflation* ("demystification") of illusory ideals, serving an exploitative status quo, is accompanied by an *expansion* of the great Game of language, in an entirely disabused spirit of modernity.

All that is true to a point, but stops short of the authentic nature of Mallarmé's revolution. Mallarmé went beyond the negation of idealism to a "new testament" of spirit—he speaks of the original myths brought by poets of his time in "Richard Wagner . . ." and *Les Dieux antiques*—and the *Jeu suprême* is magnetized by an unprecedented faith and sense of beauty, comparable, as Edmund Wilson observed, to the enthusiastic fresh view of the cosmos brought by an Einstein (who, as Valéry noted, considered himself a sort of artist and who clearly believed in a version of Spinoza's God, heedless of contemporary derision). Later, at a lower level, Camus' "sacred" moves in a parallel direction: the "center . . . buried sun" ("The Enigma"), which art approaches, is a locus of ultimate faith, objective reality. Mallarmé, unlike Valéry, never abandoned his aesthetic aims; destructive as they were of previous art—he often spoils other texts for us—he nevertheless felt the world would be "saved by literature" (quoted by Jean Royère), not just by his own but by the whole tradition, which he saw as leading up to and nourishing at the roots his crowning synthesis (*Autobiographie*, p. 661). In that way, he renews the tradition, redeems it from its misuse by a cynical society, with his "purer sense" of "the words of the tribe."

I will not go over the ground covered by such critics as Paul Bénichou and Jean-Pierre Richard, as well as myself, concerning Mallarmé's feeling of responsibility to a public and to his time. I will merely observe that he *believed*, both socially and metaphysically, in the most unsentimental manner conceivable, and that his well-known remark to Ghil, "On ne peut se passer d'Eden," and the "Oui" of *Quand l'ombre menaça* and that ultimate, distant CONSTELLATION toward—*vers*—which his human yearning for meaning points, however wistfully, tentatively, and despairingly at times, are sufficient witness of that faith.

No doubt for Mallarmé the words of *Igitur* didn't attract each other enough or complexly enough—he hadn't quite found his way to the core of his Vision, linguistically—and did not form those vibrant constellations, clusters, that together go far to define a single poetic universe in his final perspective. In the *Coup de Dés*, a word like *blanchi* opens up in all directions, not just abstractly, as part of a naked Syntax; it is poetically very present, rich, erotic, and beautiful (see *O.*, pp. 137–40 or Appendix A in *T.P.*; also Jacques Derrida's later and parallel investigations in *La Dissémination*). That being said, *Igitur* is an immensely appealing and fascinating text, largely because of its mystery, its obsessive depth of self-involvement, its pioneering suicidal absurdism, as Sartre noted in his study—and its stark beauty, with royal blacks à la Goya, Manet, Redon. In another letter to Cazalis, of July 1869, Mallarmé speaks of his project in more upbeat tones; after alluding to his bout of suffering he adds: "Si j'en peux extraire un beau conte—vous l'aurez." *Igitur* is after all a major work of Mallarmé and of our tradition.

Perhaps we can put it in these terms: Mallarmé was tremendously serious in this enterprise—it involved a struggle for survival and creative growth—and so, despite the willful and goal-oriented aspect, ad hoc (which, as Valéry after Kant and Poe noted, art isn't) he could hardly help the poetry creeping in anyway, clothing his naked story at times in svelte black lines and even spurts of whiteness, like the lace ruff in the dark or the dice, which at least hint at that later universal *blanchi* and its overtones in "Une dentelle s'abolit" and the like.

And when we think that Mallarmé has impressive claims to be the pivotal poet and thinker of the modern tradition—see "The Mallarmé Century" in *Stanford French Review*, Winter 1978—then we realize that it is high time for someone to look at the text in close detail.

As in the case of my study of the *Coup de Dés*, it

appears useful to spiral gradually toward the fullness of the complex text, beginning with a tentative, fairly superficial tour. First, let us deal with Igitur's mysterious name.

2. Wherefore "Igitur"

THE FULL TITLE of Mallarmé's metaphysical *conte*, as published in the *Oeuvres complètes*,[12] reads as follows: *Igitur ou la folie d'Elbehnon*. What the *folie* is soon becomes clear, but the name of the hero, and of his mysterious site, have puzzled many. Roland de Renéville, in *L'Expérience poétique*, has invoked a passage of the Vulgate, *igitur perfecti sunt coeli*, and has further claimed that Elbehnon (*el behnon*) refers to a Hebrew word meaning "sons of the Elohim," emissaries of the Creator. Many critics, including Guy Michaud—somewhat charily (in his *Mallarmé*)—and, more recently, Louis Bolle (in "Mallarmé, Igitur et Hamlet," a review article in *Critique*, no. 21, 1965) go along with this view. To me, this seems a dubious explanation: there is no substantiation in the text. There is not a single *donc* to echo the Biblical "therefore," nor is the spelling of *behn* a likely equivalent of the usual phonetic rendering of the Hebrew *ben*, "son." Nothing indicates a knowledge of Hebrew on Mallarmé's part or a detailed knowledge of occult lore. Mallarmé's hero, moreover, is located at the end of creation rather than at the beginning; he rebels against any creative, or demiurgic, activity whatsoever and seeks rather a reunion with solid Being, in the Manichean or Gnostic pattern.

There may well be in the name of Igitur an overtone

12. Pléiade edition of 1945. All page references without other indication are to this edition.

of "therefore," but I believe it is independent of the Vulgate expression, which is, after all, a a random occurrence. Mallarmé's putative "therefore" would simply refer to a summing-up final gesture of self-sacrifice —the "parole et geste unis" (p. 434)—involved in the blowing out of a candle of life or consciousness, leading "therefore" to a total Nothing from which Everything might be born, losing all to gain all in the Gospel sense, or Kirilov's. This might be considered a reversal of the Cartesian formula "I think therefore I am" and might explain in part the expression "Vous mathématiciens expirâtes—moi projeté absolu" (p. 434); Igitur, the opposite of Descartes, abandons all thought and might be saying "I do not think, therefore I am not."[13]

Regardless of this somewhat tenuous connection with a famous *donc*—which was rendered rather by *ergo*— the word *igitur* has an air of metaphysical nudity about it, expressing nothing but a pure relationship; it is close to mere silence or a punctuation mark or a term like *ecce* (as in *ecce homo*). One muses that Mallarmé might have called his hero *Point*, recalling the "point dernier qui sacre" of the *Coup de Dés*. Musing further, we recall that he associated a *point d'exclamation* with one of his key symbols, the feather, which plays a central role in that Poem as a "feather in the cap" of his Hamletic hero, standing for pure artistic vision:

> Ce point, Dujardin, on le met
> Afin d'imiter un plumet. (p. 168)

Here we are getting warmer. Mallarmé was highly conscious of the sounds and shapes of the letters of the

13. In his metaphysical-linguistic *Notes* (p. 851), Mallarmé refers to Descartes as one of his literary "Pères" and adds: "Il a suscité les mathématiciens français."

alphabet—we need only cite *Les Mots anglais*—and the letter *i* is the brightest acoustically, as he was well aware: "*I*, éclaircissement" (p. 983). It is also the most cleanly vertical—"virile," slim, and heroic, particularly in the capital form, as in *Igitur*. The *I* in upper case on Page 8 of the *Coup de Dés* is very much to our point. It may be worth recalling that the Hebrew *iod* was the mystic letter par excellence (the *J* of *JHVH* or *Jehovah*; Dante refers to it and its concrete, degraded form *El* in Canto XXVI of *Paradiso*). The *t* of *Igitur* is similarly vertical, the *u* is comparatively bright, the *i* is repeated (as in Villiers' *Isis*). In sound and shape, then, *Igitur* evokes a brilliant flash of vision, like the lightning stroke of the Hamlet hero on Page 7 of the *Coup de Dés*, instantly fusing earth and sky, or the similar *foudre* of Saint John's vision in *Hérodiade*, at a Midnight of the mind. Hence the probable overtone *rigide* as in "rigide en opposition au ciel," which refers to the lightning-feather-vision on the Hamlet figure's head (Page 7 of the *Coup de Dés*). In the same series of overtones is the *tige* of "la tige / Grandissait trop pour nos raisons" of *Prose* (*pour des Esseintes*) and the *vertige* of the Hamlet feather: "la lucide et seigneuriale aigrette de vertige" (Page 8). The cluster includes: "frigide-égide (loi)-exige-figer-digit" (cf. *O.*, p. 263). Also *Ci-gît*: the hero commits his psychic suicide, closes the book (on life), and "se couche sur les cendres de ses ancêtres" (p. 442). Compare:

> Ci-gît le noble vol humain
> Cendre ployée avec ces livres. (p. 162)

In the little quatrain, the *cendre* refers to the vestiges of dead ancestral geniuses symbolized in the black marks of characters in books. In *Igitur* we have an ancestral

book, "ancêtres ... subsistent les caractères du grimoire"
(p. 433), and ancestral ashes, "cendres ... celles indivises
de la famille" (p. 433). Hence it is quite possible that
when in 1894 Mallarmé put these two images together
in the little quatrain, penned to decorate the library of
a friend, he thought in passing of his youthful hero as
he wrote *Ci-gît*. Of course, this is highly speculative
but, we hope, suggestive.

Ixion, the Greek and Latin god to whom Mallarmé
devoted a chapter of *Les Dieux antiques*, attracted him
enough so that when he signed certain articles of *La
Derniére Mode* with *Ix.* we may suspect an echo of it.
The two *i*'s together with the geometric *x* give an effect
rather close to Igitur, and the tetrapolar pattern that
dominates the story fascinated Mallarmé in the myth as
well: "Reste la roue à quatre jantes d'Ixion. C'est la croix
de feu, les rayons transversaux et vibrants que voient,
dans le ciel, ceux qui regardent le soleil, à midi." That
centrality of *midi* recalls the *minuit* of *Igitur*: "Le voc-
able Ixion ... apparenté au grec *axôn* et au latin *axis*."
Villiers' *Axël* will depend largely on that effect.

Because it is generally agreed that he had Villiers very
much on his mind when he wrote *Igitur* (Edmond
Bonniot was probably the first to make this point: Villiers was *the* modern Hamlet for Mallarmé, like Axël
in his isolated castle), it is bemusing to note that in
Villiers' *Elën*—a work which wildly excited Mallarmé
(*Corr.*, p. 153)—of 1865 (Chamuel, p. 58), students are
singing the traditional *Gaudeamus igitur* and there is a
reference to the river Elbe, as perhaps in Elbehnon.
Mallarmé seems to be locating his drama in the same
suspended, vaguely Franco-German legendary region as
Poe, in his *Domain of Arnheim*, Villiers, in his metaphys-

ical plays and stories, or Maeterlinck, in *Pelléas et Mélisande* ("Allemonde").[14] In *Les Mots anglais* there is: "Des ancêtres germains . . . leurs descendants venaient d'où? Des rives de l'Elbe" (p. 905). This would be further in line with the elevated and dark site of the original Hamlet; the *El* slightly recalls the Nordic Elseneur (Elsinore) and, more importantly, the whole rhythm and flavor of Elbehnon echoes Hamlet's castle. Perhaps the *nuit ébénéenne* of *T.*II is another echo (recalling the *oiseau d'ébène* of his translation of *The Raven*). The *non* at the end adds a sombre note of negation, the very theme of the *conte*.

Still another possibility emerges from the solitary locale of that other modern Hamlet, Vathek, as described in the following passage cited by Mallarmé in his preface to his translation of William Beckford's story:

> La vieille maison de Fonthill avait l'une des plus vastes salles du royaume, haute et d'écho sonore; et des portes nombreuses y donnaient accès de différentes parties du bâtiment, par d'obscurs, de longs et sinueux corridors. C'est de là que j'ai tiré ma salle imaginaire, ou d'Eblis, engendrée par celle de ma propre résidence. (p. 552)

Eblis and Elbehnon are at least faintly related in sound and are very much related in character: the *écho*, *sonore*, and *corridors* are prominent in *Igitur*;[15] the echo *ego-écho*, implying a self-other vibrancy, was published in a list of jottings by Bonniot together with our text.

14. Here we recall the general influence of German Romanticism and specifically of Wagner.

15. It is not known when Mallarmé first became acquainted with *Vathek*, but Mondor surmises it was probably as early as his stay in England in 1862. (*Igitur* was written in the late sixties.) Beckford and his seignorial domain are mentioned in Baudelaire's translation of a Poe story in 1865 (*Poe, oeuvres en prose*, Gallimard, 1965, p. 1590).

I am not suggesting that *Igitur* and *Elbehnon* are supposed to directly evoke in the reader any of the foregoing virtualities but rather am trying to show how the names probably arose, half-spontaneously, by imaginative condensation and crystallization from the likeliest background sources. We are well aware by now that Mallarmé always worked in this convergent way in his poetry and that names participate in the process:

> Un beau nom est l'essentiel
> Comme dans la glace on s'y mire
> Céline reflète du ciel
> Juste autant qu'il faut pour sourire. (p. 149)

Or "Monsieur Fraisse n'a la frousse" (p. 174); Voltaire made him think of an arrow (*vol*; p. 872), Coppée, of a sword (*épée*; in a letter), and so on.

There is nothing unusual in this. Joyce loved to play with names in this fashion: the hero of *Finnegans Wake*, Shem, derives from Irish *Shamus*, Hebrew *Shem*, English *sham* and *shame*, etc. It has been convincingly demonstrated that dozens of Thomas Mann's characters are comparably synthetic. C. S. Lewis described the process very well in a preface to *The Screwtape Letters*.

In sum, *Igitur* and *Elbehnon* were chosen, in part at least, because they included reminiscences of Hamlet, Poe, Beckford, and Villiers and also contained effective sound and visual symbolism, as well as some interesting harmonies or overtones in the French language (including the trisyllabic "Mallarmé"). But, to repeat our earlier cautionary note, we can hardly afford to be dogmatic about any of this; eventually these are matters of ear. Names like these are not supposed to evoke, in other than the most delicately suggestive way, specific things or places. The too-pin-downable would spoil the effect, which depends precisely on this: a human being, a personality, is something more than any or all of that.

There is a further indication of why Mallarmé chose *Igitur* for his hero and title, one that will take us to the heart of his poetics and to the underlying epistemology that leads to seminal developments both in *Igitur* and in the later "cosmogonic Poem" (Paul Claudel), *Un Coup de Dés*.

First we must emphasize again how uniquely holistic is Mallarmé's characteristic art. The name of a work, for him, is the germ, the microcosm of the whole. There is no break, accordingly, between the tiniest part—even down to the letters that make up words—and the macrocosmic entirety. I have explored this aspect of his art—which today is apt to be called his "Cratylism"[16]—in extenso in my various studies. Here, *pour mémoire*, I will refer only to his remarks on why he chose *Hérodiade* for the name of his princess and the work that embodies her and much of his finest poetry:

> la plus belle page de mon oeuvre sera celle qui ne contiendra que ce nom divin Hérodiade. Le peu d'inspiration que j'ai eu, je le dois à ce nom, et je crois que si mon héroïne s'était appelée Salomé, j'eusse inventé ce mot sombre, et rouge comme une grenade ouverte, Hérodiade. Du reste, je tiens à en faire un être purement rêvé et absolument indépendente de l'histoire. (*Corr.*, p. 154)

In *Toward the Poems of Mallarmé* where I quote this (p. 53), I go on to show how the sounds and shapes of

---

16. This is the term Genette uses (after Barthes) in his *Mimologiques* (Seuil, 1976), which unfortunately completely misses the mark in its chapter on Mallarmé; see my "Mallarmé contre Genette."

the letters or groups of them lead to the imagery and the themes of the poem; delicate as the process is with its obvious dangers of arbitrariness and subjectivism, my demonstration in this specific instance nonetheless won the approval of various readers and such discriminating critics as Jean-Pierre Richard and Gérard Genette.[17]

In previous studies, I show the importance of the shape of the letter *i* versus *u* for the development of Mallarmé's cosmogonic thought: *i*, the Hebrew *iod*, as is universally recognized in occult tradition, is the phallic letter par excellence, male, vertical; *u*, with its trough or womb shape, a receptacle, is female, despite an ambiguity presented by the bright sound of the letter in French, which Mallarmé takes account of in the underlying fact of original unity between the sexual opposites. This development of male from female and reversing into female from male is the substance of Page 3 of *Un Coup de Dés* and my analysis of it. I noted the concrete biological facts behind this pattern plus some parallels from general anthropology, such as the "penis-womb" of certain tribal myths and a fascinating passage in *Finnegans Wake* (Viking, 1939, p. 76).

Now, the central thread of *Igitur* is this kind of dialectic between male idea and female unconscious (a light-dark polarity symbolized by candle and darkness of varying sorts; also an up-down polarity, etc.), and the "narrative" to a large extent is the exploration of the paradoxical reversals of one into the other. The *i* followed by *u* in *Igitur*, working at this close range to the texture of life, undoubtedly is related to the imagery and the epistemological events that *are* the story. One mysterious fragment will illustrate this point succinctly.

17. In *L'Univers imaginaire de Stéphane Mallarmé* and *Mimologiques*, respectively.

27

In chapter 4 (subtitled *Le Coup de Dés*) of *Igitur* we find this isolated phrase: "Le Cornet est la Corne de licorne—d'unicorne." A *Cornet* is a dice horn, from which the dice will be thrown; *licorne* is the usual French word for "unicorn"; *unicorne* is rather Germanic in etymology but acceptable too in French.

For our purposes, the major aspect of this mythological beast, going back 2,300 years in our tradition, is that his one horn is clearly phallic in impact—by that I mean not sexual except as undertone, precisely in the sense of *Aufhebung* or sublimation. Albertus Magnus, in his *Summa de creaturis*, comments on both aspects and links the creature with Christ, as does the bestiary tradition generally. That one horn points to the stars, or a star, as does all aspiration—an implication, in occult tradition, is that it is the male instrument of thought-stars (Richard, *L'Univers imaginaire de Stéphane Mallarmé*, p. 216) —and that will have some bearing on later developments of the symbol in Mallarmé (the stars as cosmic dice thrown from a horn in the *Coup de Dés*). But the main point is simply that it is an aspiring unity, as opposed to a duality, as in the expression "The (two) horns of a dilemma," and hence a profound symbol of resolution, of overcoming the linear duality of Becoming in favor of a triumphant singularity, as in countless texts of our mystic heritage.

When, as in the delicate medieval portrayals, the Christ-like unicorn lays its head in the lap of the virgin who alone can tame him, Albertus Magnus sees the horn as subtly transformed into a pure instrument of insemination, echoing the divine birth. That inversion of the male into docile female—the proud horn now pointed down—is linked subtly with the fact that man becomes female in his inversions, sometimes physically but certainly psychically. His aggressions become submissions, as Hercules dons the garb of Omphale. In love, the male moves to the female pole of reality, becoming feminine to a degree, is even "castrated" by the sexual act, as the analysts see it. In the medieval *Lai d'Aristote* the love-girl rides on the sage's back.

Thus male horn becomes female dice horn, a simple physical confirmation.[18] Wave becomes trough; father becomes mere site—foundered boat, a sort of male womb —for his rising son, at the bottom of Page 4: he is called a "naufrage direct de l'homme," referring to sexual perpetuation, the "petite mort," and the total death that may lead to life on the next page, the page of the son, a "shadow" very like Igitur, a little Hamlet figure, as a wave rises from the preceding trough.

That duality is a prime symbol of femininity for Mallarmé is shown at length in my various studies;[19] the twin sides of the little trough, for example, in the letter *u* or feminine "lips." This prepares us to understand why Mallarmé plays, in the little isolated phrase, with the following: the *Corne* and the *Cornet* are precisely a male-female pair, as we have shown, and are dialectically related in their similarity. More elusively, the pair *licorne* and *unicorne* contain the *i* to *u* shift in the names of the creature, the same shift we have in the name *Igitur* and in the substance of the text itself.

Mallarmé used the unicorn image in one other major

---

18. Which paradox fascinates Derrida in the shape of the *pli*; I had noted the development of the *pli* in that sense in *O.* and *T.P.*, but as part of a universal process encompassing many other aspects of the inversion.

19. For example, in *T.P.*, p. 264.

context: *Ses purs ongles*, from roughly the same period as *Igitur*.[20] There, on the mirror frame in the dark Midnight chamber, where the departure of a poet (or Master) leaves a purity, as in *Igitur*, we see:

Des licornes ruant du feu contre une nixe

The unicorns with their gold (the *or* is an effective element in the word) on the frame, and "kicking" its gilt "fire," are in contrast to the mirror-cold and watery nymph or "nixie." Mallarmé often thought of the liquid mirror as a feminine essence, as in *Hérodiade* or in *Frisson d'hiver*, where he "sinfully" sees the vague image of a nude woman, who formerly "bathed" her narcissistic beauty there; here, in the sonnet, she is a *défunte nue*, ambiguously cloud and nude.[21]

In *Ses purs ongles* there is a mysterious shell-like object, a *ptyx* whose ghost is left behind on a sideboard or "credenza"; it is a fragile relic, such as the *faux manoir* evanescently remaining as the monument of mankind in the *Coup de Dés*. Most importantly for our present viewpoint, in emphasis, at least, it inverts: first it sits in absentia on the credenza; then "le Maître est allé puiser des pleurs au Styx / Avec ce seul objet dont le Néant s'honore." I show, in my study (*T.P.*, pp. 138–46), the parallels in the shape of the Big Dipper, which haunted

20. See also *N.*, p. 128, where a unicorn, frightened, figures on a mysterious tapestry.

21. Mallarmé liked to play with the battle of the sexes, for example, in *Mes Bouquins refermés* and his interview on female cyclists. According to Camille Soula (*Gloses sur Mallarmé*, Editions Diderot, 1946, p. 139), Mallarmé got his image from Heine's *De l'Allemagne*, where there is a combat of unicorns and nixies. For further references to the *licorne*, see Richard, pp. 215–16.

Mallarmé in the major Poem, pivoting like a doffed headgear (Page 7), as well as in the sonnet.

To doff the hat is a gesture of male pride become submission. Hamlet's lightning-emitting and -attracting toque and its total inversion to folly—*toqué*—are an important image in the *Coup de Dés*, Page 7. The feather, *plume solitaire éperdue*, fixed rigidly in its *toque de minuit* is the peak of this process, echoing Igitur's midnight Instant. It inverts with the hat, or bends over like the feather in a fool's cap, and plummets head-down into the ocean of *folie*. The pivoting of the Big Dipper is therewith suggested in a way children would appreciate: they are wont to put saucepans on their heads as helmets.[22]

---

22. Hamlet's madness is linked with a major Renaissance topos involving the melancholia phase of the four humors, parallel to the "symphonic equation" that Mallarmé saw as expressive of the cycle of moods as well as yearly seasons (p. 646). From some unidentified emblematic source, Banville derived:

> Le vent qui fait voler ta plume noire
> Et te caresse, Hamlet, ô jeune Hamlet! (p. 299)

But Delacroix and Manet, depicting the actor Faure, present a black toque with a white feather, as does Villiers in his *Premières poésies* (Lacomblez, 1893, p. 62) and *Isis* (Crès, 1923, p. 219). See also *O.*, p. 258.

The inversion of a proud mentality is expressed in such phrases as *travailler du chapeau*, "mad as a hatter," "madcap," and the like. See Thomas Hanson, "Mallarmé's Hats," in *Yale French Studies*, no. 54, 1977, pp. 215–27. The theme of inversion goes back to the original metaphysical crest and trough from which Mallarmé's cosmogony derives (*O.*, pp. 51–60). Derrida based a famous passage of *La Dissémination* (Seuil, 1972), on the *pli* in this sense of a 2-1 paradox. The extent to which I had preceded him is evident in this passage from *L'Oeuvre de Mallarmé: Un Coup de Dés* (p. 261):

The inversion occurs also in the final poem, *Un Coup de Dés*, when the *faux manoir* turns upside down like the drowning siren diving from her ephemeral rock: there, as we show (*O.*, p. 335), the *i* shape becomes a *u* and the neighboring *y* shape of her disappearing tail as proud unity becomes the flux of duality and eventually the evaporation of all reality.

Confirmation of this effect is readily found in English: *big, rise, high, prick, I, right* versus *slump, sulk, skulk, bum, dump, rump, sump* . . . (See also *O.*, pp. 94–96, 102–3, 108–9.)

Mallarmé's liminal outline for *Igitur* ("A peu près . . ."; C) begins with *le Minuit*, the image of *l'Horloge* at its mysterious end of cycle and beginning, death and resurrection. Later, Igitur says "J'ai toujours vécu mon âme fixée sur l'horloge" (III, O).

When staring at a clock at midnight one sees a single upright slim figure, two become one,[23] which is the union of opposites mystics have always sought, the "reployer la division" of the *Coup de Dés*. It is like a finger, or a phallic figure—the "petite raison virile / contenue"

"par un rhythme de phrase . . . comme d'un pli de robe" (861). "Le pli de sombre dentelle qui retient l'infini, tissé par mille" (1565) indique ainsi un sens important de *sombre*, la noirceur de l'encre. Il est à peine nécessaire d'ajouter qu'un pli de l'écriture est une petite émanation finale de la Crête et du Creux originels, et le *ptyx* de *Ses purs ongles* . . . (etym. *pli*) illustre les mêmes inversions et girations paradoxales qui se développeront bientôt ici. . . .

23. Cf. the steeple as the "finger of God" in *Du côté de chez Swan* (Gallimard, 1954, p. 66). Two of them (and three) become one, as in the Trinity, as little Marcel rides in the carriage with Dr. Percepied, in Proust's miraculous little piece of prose, written at age fourteen. Note that in the *douze* of the successful *coup* of *Igitur*, section V, there are a 1 and 2 (12).

of the *Coup de Dés*—with its little conical hat, standing on a circular dot of base, as in the *prince amer de l'écueil* image—recalling Hamlet on his "sterile promontory," the global base of earth.

L'Horloge is the final poem of the "Spleen et Idéal" section, the major section by far, of *Les Fleurs du mal*, the poetic work which most influenced Mallarmé. It begins:

> Horloge! dieu sinistre, effrayant, impassible,
> Dont le doigt nous menace. . . .

The vertical finger, annunciatory or forbidding (like the lifted sword of the angel at the gate of paradise)[24] as so often in Mallarmé,[25] is echoed by an exclamation mark and a series of *i*'s, as in our commentary above. It goes on:

> *Souviens-toi* que le Temps est un joueur avide
> Qui gagne sans tricher, à tout coup! c'est la loi.

And, in the final strophe:

> Tantôt sonnera l'heure où le divin Hasard . . .
> Où tout te dira: Meurs, vieux lache! il est trop tard.

That *Temps*, *coup* of a *joueur* (*coup de dés*; cf. Baudelaire's poem *Le Jeu*), and *Hasard*, which has the last word—as in the already-quoted crucial passage on *l'absurde* in *Igitur*—along with other influences, must have worked powerfully on Mallarmé's imagination at this time of his life. They are central images of *Igitur*. And, to repeat, it is probable that the rigid, little, single phallic figure of the clock hand(s) at Midnight has some-

24. See my commentary on *Le Tombeau d'Edgar Poe* in *T.P.*, pp. 153–57.
25. *Ouverture ancienne d'Hérodiade*, *Sainte*, translation of *Ulalume* . . .

thing to do with our hero; standing up in, and to, the round encompassing matrix of the cosmic astral dial.

3. Outline

THE SCHEMA of the narrative is this:

I. *Le Minuit*: A Midnight of the mind in which a sacrificial resolve is made: to die, at least spiritually, in order to Live.

II. *L'Escalier*: The Hero goes down into the unconscious in order to go up to an infinite Idea.

III. *La Vie d'Igitur*: He looks back over the past evolution leading to this moment.

IV. *Le Coup de dés* (au tombeau): He performs the momentous "suicidal" gesture, a dice throw of fate.

V. *Il se couche au tombeau*: This tiny passage tells of the result.

Essentially, epistemologically, the foregoing can be summed up on a Cartesian cross as follows:

I. An absolute, zero-infinite (micro-macro), at the core of the drama, a resolve fixed in space to a zero point (the clock "diamond") and in time, likewise, at a static "midnight" (the "infinite" is the cosmic whole that is at stake, the blown-up, macrocosmic version of the core).

II. A vertical paradox of fall to rise, of body-mind, etc.

III. A horizontal paradox of the diachronic, past-future, explored.

IV. A return, spirally, to the first absolute (zero-infinite), this time not merely to contemplate this resolve but to act upon it, make a gesture that will embody it as a part of the universal Becoming, or part of Creation. This is the "dice throw."

v. The result of the gesture (rather ambiguous, tentative).

The basic drama of *Igitur* is a series of attempts to overcome, in a Manichean pattern, the becoming-linearity of life, or what he refers to as "l'omniprésente Ligne" in *La Musique et les lettres*; the goal is a perfect Being, round like the "lune au-dessus du temps" (*Ancienne Étude*). An obvious target, then, is the irreversibly linear aspect of fleeting time, as in the above-mentioned *Horloge* of Baudelaire. Here one easily recalls the Proust of *À la recherche du temps perdu*, who in a privileged moment discovers an eternity "hors du temps." Thinkers from Aristotle through Nietzsche, Mallarmé, and Rimbaud to J. Dunne have noted that the one-way movement of time is an arbitrary conception, not at all demonstrable within the system; one doesn't *feel* any movement at all, and in visionary moments, on the contrary, one feels a *totum simul*,[26] a great simultaneity of all, as Nietzsche did in his rhapsodic description of the "Eternal Return." We know, ordinarily, that we are born and die, two points defining a line. But we sense, intuitively and wholly, from the model of the time-telling sun, that it all goes around invisibly and comes back. Our time devices reflect this ambiguity of circular-linear, which runs through all our reality, aspects of the dialectic of vertical-metaphoric-whole and horizontal-metonymic-fragmented. So we may sense too the reason for Plato's doctrine of reincarnation in the *Meno*,

26. See G. Poulet, *Études sur le temps humain*, I: 400–1.

or the Buddhist equivalent, or Kierkegaard's "repetition," and the like.

The "reployer la division" (*Coup de Dés*) of life makes two back into one, as in the mystic and poetic tradition of the union of contraries: the Platonic myth of the androgyne, the biblical lamb and lion, the rose and fire of *The Divine Comedy*; Shakespeare's alchemical union of fire and water in the sonnets; Donne's likewise; Baudelaire's fusion of sunlight and water in *La Chevelure*, Rimbaud's "mer mêlée avec le soleil" (*L'Éternité*); Mallarmé's restless *jeu* between motion and rest, cold and hot, etc., in all his work;[27] Proust's "alliteration" between the minnow jar (stasis) and the flowing Vivonne river (kinesis); the night and day "ceasing to be perceived as contraries" of Breton; and so on throughout our finest literature.

And so *Igitur* tries to stop time's flow in various ways: by shutting himself up hermetically—with drapes drawn —in a silent room where nothing moves, including himself, "collecting the least particle of time"; by staring fixedly into a mirror in the near dark, as we all have done, in an effort, precisely, to seize our reality, our Being. This ordeal without diversion is *ennuyeux* in the extreme and is another homeopathic device for dealing with the ennui and sterility Mallarmé was suffering from; i.e., "you're bored," he might be saying to himself, "nah, here's boredom for you, take it until it or you can't take any more and you'll be cured." Just sweat it out, live it down . . .

When one stares fixedly at one's image in a mirror long enough the boredom (horizontally) may turn into horror (vertically) as the habitual and familiar gives

27. See my "Mallarmé's Windows."

way to the monstrously unfamiliar, at too-close range—animal, vegetable impressions as in such a moment of *La Nausée* or *Le Mythe de Sisyphe*, experiences of the absurd—and, worse, begins to break up, especially in the near-dark. That mixture of boredom and horror in the mirror is part of the psychic suicide.

At a certain dread point there is a leap into a sort of absolute, "out of time," a death-rebirth; one feels Olympian, "impersonal," as the text notes—the "impersonnel," "une aptitude qu'a l'univers spirituel à se voir" (letter to Cazalis, 14 May 1867, *Corr.*, p. 242)—as in Nietzsche's similar experience of "obedience to the cosmos." Then things seem to become authentic, themselves; the furniture in the room becomes "fixed," objective in that sense.

Igitur is thus "projeté hors du temps" as time drops into a sort of tomb, with him figuratively lying there—as he will at the end of the story in a gesture of burial; this is called "la chute de l'heure," and the tomb doors close on it definitively, as in *Toast funèbre* with its equally stoic emphasis, its pagan denial of sentimental religious hope for an afterlife.

In this absolute condition—this "présent absolu des choses"—the ghostly apparition of his face and of a page from an open book seem to represent authentic survivals, images of rebirth. The image of all outdoors in the evoked sea and sky (suggested by the touches of the gleaming clock frame, like sheer phenomena of waves or stars as in various of the poems) is the macrocosmic original Creation, which the potential creation of the brain behind the face and page will emulate or "repeat" —in the Kierkegaardian sense—authentically.

But first Igitur relives the history of his race, as Mallarmé said he himself would do in the quoted letter to

Cazalis: this is the diachronic, sketchily essential Becoming dimension we find throughout his work, even in the small poems, culminating in the *ancestralement* that sums up the cosmic and human evolution leading to the supreme encounter with fate in the *Coup de Dés*, as here, in a final gesture by a late son of humanity, a poet, guess who.

The imagery develops as follows: the pendulum of the clock, as in Poe, is associated with a heartbeat. That duality is in turn linked with a wing-beat.[28] These dualities may be summed up in a vertical polarity of up-down, as in a binary beat of music (or the more complex extension into systole-diastole) or as we see it on a cardiogram, as simply rhythm. Horizontally it becomes, through time, a series, successive shadows of his ancestors. The fundamental past-future line of all time sums up the horizontal polarity that together with the vertical forms a tetrapolarity, concretized in a four-walled room, the symmetry of which, "reflecting" (there is an elaborate image of four-polar—and, fleetingly, even polypolar —reflection) the epistemological one, satisfies Igitur at some point that he has indeed reached a stasis of perfection, coincidence with the all.[29]

28. This feather movement (a *frottement* or *frôlement*, at times) is associated—as in fragments of the *Noces* concerning the nurse (*N.*, p. 60) and in the activity of Mallarmé's wife in *Éventail*—with that of a housekeeper's feather duster, sweeping away the dust that is the visible sign of time. In essence, the idea is of Becoming as an *Ewig-Weibliche*, a feminine on-going wave movement, the duality, which is a feminine essence for Mallarmé (see *T.P.*, p. 264), sweeping out the old and bringing in the new.

29. Various other symmetries are involved: a highly conscious–highly unconscious polarity (Igitur being both above and below the sentimental horizontal line of his ancestors—he salvages the [double] unconscious idea that was latent from the

At that point, when he is at one with, or at home in, the world, he can make a gesture that is the world's and that will be an authentic act of creation. He makes it, the supreme dice throw that is the image of all creativity, or, as he says in the later definitive masterwork: "Toute Pensée émet un Coup de Dés" (Page 11). The impersonal mind of man, the "thing" of creation, gives off an object, a phenomenon-child of the flesh-spirit, which is tossed about—like Vigny's textual "bottle in the sea"—by the laws of chance and becoming governing all the rest.

In the later work, as we said, the odds are far greater, everything is more hesitant, elusive, anguishing, tentative, and staved-off.

Time is normally pictured (e.g., in graphs) as a horizontal dimension, space as a vertical. If we imagine a Cartesian coordinate graph with these axes crossed, we can see that the attempt to freeze time to a central zero point of origin (round like Being, a microcosm of it, a Nothing-All) is related to a similar attempt on the vertical axis that will reduce the linearity of space to a point, the same one. This is the essence of the dialectic of the candle and the book, the black print on the white page, the light and the dark, and so on (cf. the two clock hands becoming one at Midnight, the paradoxical zero point of the end of cycle). Mallarmé in various texts—*L'Après-midi d'un faune*, *Une dentelle s'abolit*—speaks of a line of writing as a sort of *blasphème*, just as Rousseau thought of the first fence as a sort of biblical snake di-

---

beginning and was delayed until him) is crossed by a horizontal version of itself (Igitur as conscious versus the ancestors as unconscious, including an unconscious version of himself). This will be developed in detail later.

viding man from paradise. The famous white page represents, macrocosmically, the ultimate perfectionism of his style, which reduces all prolixity, microcosmically, to a near-nothing, extreme reserve, French discretion, or *pudeur*; as we noted earlier, the macrocosmic absolute —perfection of the whole—is dialectically related to the zero-nothing or the core, microcosmically. Of course, as in the calculus, Mallarmé's art merely approaches asymptotically this perfection-whole-zero; his great poems hover like the last passionate constellations on the threshold of diving—as in black hole theory—into that final point represented in the *Coup de Dés* by the North Star toward (*vers*) which they merely point with a providentially alive—on-going, feminine—inconclusiveness: *felix culpa*. This is the wise lesson Mallarmé draws in *Le Pitre châtié* where, after Poe, he decides that the tricks of the trade and the all-too-human are necessary to art. He makes much the same point in "Crise de vers" concerning the post-Babel state of language; words do not themselves, in our fallen time, directly represent things as they once are felt to have done, as in Plato's *Cratylus* and a long tradition. That too is providential for the poet, who makes up for the loss through his art, which restores the old unions.

But in certain moments of his poetry, e.g., *Don du poème* or *Brise marine*, the addiction to perfection seems to win out, and the poet just stares for a while at the white page, defeated, like a sulking child who looks back into the paradise of the womb (micro) or, before, the all (macro; an all-womb) and refuses to come forth—as do all true poets at times. It is as if the line—or its extension into the threads of the lacework that is his image for the network of universal analogy linking all his best work into one great universe of the imagination—had been progressively erased and at last merged with the page. This is the idea behind the important imagery of blowing out the candle by which the book (*grimoire*) is read and the cognate theme of erasing the dots from the dice, leaving only a "Château de la pureté." In all these cases, as we said, the linearity of space is reduced to a (round) zero, or wholeness, perfection of Being, micro and macro.

The more complex dialectic of various fragments involves not just a bipolar dilemma—linearity to be overcome—on one dimension, but the two dimensions of our cross together, dialectically (paradoxically, interchangeably) related in what we call tetrapolarity. This is the true core of *Igitur*, which we will discuss in the next section. Suffice it to say here that the wrestling among the four (and multiple) poles of the drama of existence produces wakes of intellect on the page not unlike those ghostly traces in the cloud chambers of modern physics:

> Quelle agonie, aussi, qu'agite la Chimère versant par ses blessures d'or l'évidence de tout l'être pareil, nulle torsion vaincue ne fausse ni ne transgresse l'omniprésente Ligne espacée de tout point à tout autre pour instituer l'idée; sinon sous le visage humain, mystérieuse, en tant qu'une Harmonie est pure. (p. 648)

Here, despite the "golden" glimpses of total Meaning through chinks ("wounds") in the *Chimère* that tantalizes Man in his death-struggle to understand it all, Mallarmé in a later essay, *La Musique et les lettres*, despairs of any idea prevailing against the absurd (or, as a scientist might say, the "indeterminacy principle") whereby any act—*l'omniprésente Ligne*—of intellect ipso facto gets in the way of truth, no matter how many agonizing "twists" he overcomes, no matter how sophisticated, how paradoxical and polypolar the writhings of his writings (he notes this echo in *Les Mots anglais*).

But in *Igitur*, at least in most of the fragments, he seemed to hope that by a sort of willess will—cf. "céder l'initiative aux mots" (p. 366)—getting out of his own way, as it were, he could somehow win. Well, that tacit "Harmony"—preceded by a defeat subsumed behind the back of will, so to speak, as in Hegel, where *something* wins ultimately in a faithful and humble perspective nearing the Edenic—comes to much the same thing, I suppose, but the tone is significantly different, more maturely or humanly resigned and sweet.

All these motifs involve a painfully deep, sacrificial gesture; the final or crowning one is the psychic suicide of blowing out the candle of life (as in *Macbeth*), erasing that total line from the purity of the infinite. But that too seems too dramatic and willed, in retrospect, almost heavy-footed, for Mallarmé.[30]

4. Polypolarity

THE FOLLOWING OUTLINE of the concept of polypolarity is taken from my *Modes of Art* (1975); a previous formulation will be found in *L'Oeuvre de Mallarmé: Un Coup de Dés* (and its earlier version in English, 1949), but I believe the one I have chosen is the most useful for present purposes. The concept is further explored in the works mentioned, especially *Modes of Art*, in all sorts of applications. As I show in "The Mallarmé Century," this epistemology lies at the heart of the char-

---

30. Cf. Sartre's unfinished fragment of a final volume of his novel series *Les Chemins de la liberté*. We do not wonder much that Sartre had trouble going on with that . . .

acteristic ideas of our time, as has more or less been acknowledged by Roland Barthes, Michel Foucault, Sartre, and others ("all we do is repeat Mallarmé," Barthes). The most difficult texts of Structuralism, for example—Jacques Lacan, Foucault, et al.—can be understood better if it is appreciated how much they depend on a mutation from the bipolar to the bi-dimensional (paradoxical) perspective, i.e., what we call "tetrapolarity." The first major application of the epistemology, aside from the unpublished *Igitur*, was the sketch of the Great Work, the *Coup de Dés*; Mallarmé had previously announced this in his outline of the future Work with his "symphonic equation proper to the seasons" (*La Musique et les lettres*). An important result is the new emphasis on the whole page, as in music.

Reflective men have long known, since the time of Plato and before, that we apprehend the world through the interplay of opposed phenomena, or polarities. These can be theoretically arranged in twos or fours or sixes and so on, in a total epistemological purview that might be called polypolarity, or multipolarity. The latter term, multipolarity, has the advantage of being found in dictionaries, though only the engineers and physical scientists seem to have had any use for it until recently; George Kennan and some others are using it currently, I was rather surprised to note, in reference to global politics.

We will be speaking of just a single phase, the four-polar one, quadripolarity (as the engineers call it, mingling Greek and Latin roots), or tetrapolarity. The latter term was used by Robert Champigny for the first time that I know of in an article commenting on my early study of Mallarmé ("Mallarmé's Relation to Platonism and Romanticism," *MLR* 51 [1954]: 352), and, since it seemed more attractive than the dictionary's hybrid, I have adopted it and favored it ever since.

Tetrapolarity, as a distinct concept with its own set of properties, is very old in recorded thought. For example, there was the division of the ancient city into four quarters, representing four complementary human types (echoed in Plato's *Republic*); this has been illuminated in a modern study by John W. Perry, *Lord of the Four Quarters*. Other examples are the four causes of Aristotle's *Metaphysics*, the four elements of the pre-Socratics, the four cardinal points, the four evangelists, and the four mystic letters of the Hebrew tetragrammaton. To be sure, not all these patterns, even less all formulations of them, are equally lucid and consistent, but they do all represent a powerful archetype, or mental structure, that goes back far indeed in our tradition. More pertinent to our discussion is the modern consciousness of the phenomenon beginning with a pupil of Schelling named Troxler (see A. Béguin, *L'Âme romantique et le rêve*, pp. 91–93), a scant mention in Eliphas Lévi's *Dogme et rituel de la haute magie*, Kierkegaard's "absolute paradox" in *Philosophic Nothings*, and, particularly, the metaphysico-critical musings of Mallarmé. The concept is at the heart of the "symphonic equation proper to the seasons" that Mallarmé announced in his *La Musique et les lettres* (p. 646) as the core of a future Great Work, to be written by himself or somebody else. When the jottings entitled *Le Livre* were issued by Gallimard (in 1957, edited by J. Scherer), the sketches in Mallarmé's hand made the matter abundantly clear. From that point on, the case has been well established. For example, Suzanne Bernard, in her *Mallarmé et la musique*, speaks of *Le Livre* as confirming the "structure quadripolaire" of his work (Nizet, 1959, p. 143).

After Mallarmé, one could cite Jung,[31] René Guénon, Mircea Eliade, or, more exotically, Alexander Syrkine and V. N. Toporov, a pair of Soviet linguists whose article "La Triade et la Tétrade" appeared in *Tel Quel*, no. 35, and clearly influenced its editor, Philippe Sollers. Closer to home is Jacques Derrida who, in *La Dissémination* (Seuil, 1972), candidly demonstrates the considerable influence of Mallarmé's visionary thinking upon the work of Sollers and himself. He specifically mentions the word *tetrapolarity* (p. 293) and suggests a further discussion of it in the future.

In Mallarmé, the concept reached an important stage: mystic spontaneity and rootedness are combined with high critical consciousness. The indescribable is somehow described, as Bertrand Russell said of Wittgenstein's "pictures."

At its visionary base, tetrapolarity involves a full paradox: the four poles are all the same and yet different. Traditionally, paradox has been described in bipolar terms, for example, Zeno's paradox between continuity and discontinuity or the modern formulations of "the absurd."[32] But Mallarmé, after Kierkegaard, went one crucial step farther. To repeat, in a fully visionary tetrapolarity, the four poles are the same and yet different.

31. The mandala, the four types, etc. (*Archetypes and the Unconscious*, Pantheon Books, 1959). Some commentators have seen this pattern as the very hallmark of his work.

32. Or of the problem of identity: if we say $A = A$, by the time we have pronounced the second A, even the first A is no longer the same (it is altered in time), no matter how infinitely small the interval.

North, South, East, and West are really all projections (*ex-stases*) from a microcosmic zero-infinite point in the middle; when they fully converge there, they lose their identities, their "direction," as they do in the macrocosmic order of outer space. "Far out," we say, there are no directions (or at least very problematic ones), as in the delirium of Mallarmé's *Autre éventail*: "sans chemin." The vertical and horizontal dimensions turn out to be one and the same, as well as distinct, if we imagine distantly enough, as in Einstein's "curved universe" or the Husserlian concept of intersubjectivity.

We may put it this way: in a standard paradox—say Zeno's—the two poles are vibrantly related. In a tetrapolar paradox, the two axes are also vibrantly related. Or here is another approach: take any classic philosophic proposition, such as "man is free." From the viewpoint of ordinary paradox, that proposition is both true and false. But from the viewpoint of tetrapolarity, the statement that says a proposition is both true and false is itself both true and false. Thus one may speak of paradox squared, to the third power, and so on.

The fundamental propositions of modern physics are readily put in these terms. As in Zeno's paradox, time and space are both continuous and discontinuous, circular and linear. The standard diagram of relativity theory (e.g., Eddington's "hour glass") simplifies space to a single dimension crossed by the time dimension, which is dialectically related to it in the way I have just outlined: every move away from the now to a future in time is also a move to an elsewhere in space, so that we speak of a combined here-now event or, totally, of space-time. The core proposition of relativity is, in sum, a tetrapolar relation in our epistemological terms; the tetrapolar paradox of the micro, at the point of intersection that is the here-now "event," is mirrored[33] by the tetrapolar paradox of total space-time in the macro realm of the "cos-

33. "Mirrored by" implies a vibrant relation between micro and macro, zero and infinite. Indeed, it is only at the limit-juncture of the infinitely small that totality can become a new version of itself (the "operations" of Mallarmé, "transformations" of Valéry, "metamorphoses" of Malraux, "kaleidoscopic" changes of Proust, "originality" in a deep sense, etc.); a total retooling can occur only through a sort of death, reduction to the near-zero point. At that point conversion occurs; for example, religious verticality cuts across the normal flow as in *The Death of Ivan Ilyich*, or Camus' "sacred" cuts across the runaway "horizontal religions" (secular ideology) of our time. But note that the zero is only asymptotically approached, as in differential calculus: the derivative of a function is obtained only as the independent variable *approaches* zero; otherwise the derivative would itself always be a zero, useless, unlivable. Likewise Camus' apparently balanced weighing of life versus death in *Le Mythe de Sisyphe* is, when speaking, tilted toward life as long as the speaker is alive; there is a "joker in the deck." This arational tilt is the Achilles heel of his reasoning, his potential "leap," a point at which grace—faith, mercy, the "sacred" that will provide a limit to the too-perfect absurdist reasoning that kills—flows into his system. Hence, too, though life is totally ambivalent in his early work, in *La Peste* "there is more to admire . . . than despise."

Further examples of tetrapolarity include: the "four forces" of the latest physics (gravity, electromagnetism, strong force, weak force); the core of organic chemistry (C surrounded by four R's); Baudelaire, "What is pure art according to the modern conception? It is to create a suggestive magic containing at once the subject and the object, the world outside the artist and the artist himself" ("L'Art philosophique," *Oeuvres complètes*, Gallimard, 1954, p. 926; my translation); Thomas Mann, "In illness . . . elements of health are at work, and elements of illness, working geniuslike, are carried over into health" (*Doctor Faustus*, Knopf, 1948, p. 354); Freud's "four people" in the couple; the relation of the geometric dimensions in the logarithmic series; the intimate (fused) relation of horizontal and vertical in the calculus; the four basic functions of arithmetic; the "north-south" hypothetical magnetic pair complementing the electron-positron pair in contemporary physics.

mos": curved space-time (i.e., both linear and circular
in a complicated sense). It is hardly surprising then that
the quanta of Bohr should reflect both extremes (micro
and macro) in a linear-circular paradox of wave and cor-
puscle. By now the contemporary physicist is fairly be-
wildered by these proliferating paradoxes, exfoliating in
the pattern of what we call "polypolarity."

As Aristotle had long ago seen, we now can see the
danger of an infinite regress in this direction within our
epistemology. A way out from the vertigo is supplied
by the simple capacity to mutter "the heck with it" and
go about one's business in the usual human way of daily
impulse, blind faith.[34] Until another burst of restlessness,
Satanic pride, or professional distortion sends us back
again and again, into that maelstrom. Why? As Joyce
sighed: such me. But, having gone down that spiral intestinal staircase, with a lamp in our hands, at the bottom of that giddy pit we sometimes are heartened by
fellow feeling, awareness that others have been there before us, philosophical or literary "Kilroys," like Poe,
Hugo, Baudelaire, Mallarmé, Yeats. Moreover, once
back at the surface we blink at things in a new light of
understanding. *Sursum corda*!

It should be noted that the static form of tetrapolarity,
a cross in which the poles are interchangeable, is com-
plemented by a diachronic form, as in Mallarmé's sea-
son-equation, i.e., an emanation of the circular cross to
a spiral becoming, along a time dimension. In this direction of tetrapolarity, the left-middle pole can be seen
as what I have called "antisynthesis," i.e., a fourth term
added to the classic three of Plato and Hegel. Derrida

34. Whence also such constants as the absolutes (speed of
light, absolute time and space) of relativity theory.

and Julia Kristeva have taken note of this phenomenon; Kristeva claims it is present already in Hegel's *Logic*, in the final pages. At most it is a ghostly suggestion there. The concept reaches full force only with Kierkegaard and, particularly, Mallarmé. Jean Hippolyte concurs in this view of the poet's step beyond Hegel, in an article "Le *Coup de Dés* de Mallarmé et le message" (*Études philosophiques*, no. 4, Oct.-Dec. 1958, pp. 463–68).

5. Syntactic Synopsis

IN THE FOLLOWING brief, but essential, résumé of the initial fragments of *Igitur* as presented by Bonniot, we are interested primarily in the armature or development of the thought pattern. The page numbers, as usual, refer to the Pléiade edition, but the reader can follow the text conveniently in the present book by leafing ahead to Part II.

In the word *folie* of the title we have the germ of the whole *conte*; the *folie*, or, as it is also called, the *absurde*, is the drama that is played before "l'Intelligence du lecteur qui met les choses en scène, elle-même" (p. 433). The vibration or oscillation of opposites in paradox is the rhythmic development of the drama itself—like the *jeu* between the *au-delà* and the *ici-bas* in *La Musique et les lettres* (the *Jeu suprême* of all reality, as in *Une dentelle s'abolit* and the *Coup de Dés*).

The first part, *Ancienne Étude*, very fragmentary, illustrates the thought pattern only loosely, in a crude but instructive way. A polarity,[35] not yet a true vibra-

---

35. Other elements of the drama are first presented as a mere static list like a dramatis personae.

tion, is set up between a candle and a book: light (candle or page) versus dark (letters or general shadow). This duality mars the unity or the absolute, which can perhaps be achieved by blowing out the candle. Igitur —cf. the parallel in the Gospels—will lose all to gain all, the absolute. He will lose all by accepting negation—psychic death, *hasard* (later, in the subordinate forms of *ombre* and a "horizontal" form of death, *temps*, related to *ennui*)—and, as an extension, by denying immortality: "Comme il aura parlé selon l'absolu qui nie l'immortalité, l'absolu existera en dehors." In this he is different from his sentimental ancestors (who prepare his almost messianic coming with the prediction in the *grimoire*): "Igitur, tout enfant, lit son devoir à ses ancêtres." Hence here and in later fragments the crucial act is accompanied by *neutralité, indifférence, pas [de] sentiment*.

To sum up: the light-dark of candle-book is a simple concretization of positive and negative poles. The attempt to cancel these polar opposites in order to create a unity itself involves a positive-negative polarity, i.e., the polarity is polarized: as in the Platonic and Hegelian triad, positive-negative is negated to achieve a positive result. At first this is not yet a true tetrapolarity (implying equilibrium): the second polarity is incomplete since the first passage ends on a provisional note of triumph and is thus one-sidedly positive. But the rest of *Igitur* records the vibrations or dynamic equilibrium of this second polarity (Absolute versus Death),[36] which

36. This fourth term is what I have termed "antisynthesis": cf. *Modes of Art*, pp. 29–30; Kristeva, *La Révolution du langage poétique*; also Derrida, *La Dissémination*, Introduction and p. 293.

will be, momentarily at least, clearly recognized as a dilemma or *l'absurde*.

In *Le Minuit*, a finished section, the deed is presented as accomplished, at least provisionally: the light-dark duality (here the candle is presented as the *or* of this *Minuit*) has been canceled; which conception is symbolized as positive or *lumière* (as opposed to negative or dark), but since this unity cannot be conceived without creating *ipso facto* a duality (unity as opposed to multiplicity, or victory as opposed to defeat, etc.) and since, on the other hand, the mind can immediately cancel this new duality, etc., etc., an infinite regress is begun:

> C'est le rêve pur d'un Minuit, en soi disparu [opposites canceled, UNITY] et dont la Clarté reconnue, qui seule demeure au sein de son accomplissement plongé dans l'ombre [Clarté = conception (of unity-purity) = later phase of the original light, and it "remains," *demeure*, as an imperfection creating DUALITY].... Depuis longtemps morte [UNITY] une antique idée [DUALITY] se mire telle à la clarté . . . [et] elle s'invite, pour terminer l'antagonisme de ce songe polaire, à se rendre . . . au Chaos[37] de l'ombre [UNITY] [etc., etc.]. (pp. 435–36)

For the moment this series or regress is linear and will become assimilated to the flight of a bird alternately opening and closing its wings and the systole-diastole of the heartbeat.[38] But interwoven with the linear notion

37. Note that the UNITY is a cancellation, a chaos, a union of opposites: it is a negation only potentially as the negative pole of a potential second polarity.

38. Also, the movement of a feather duster wielded by genius-ancestors ridding the "thought chamber" (their mind) of clutter, dust, and spiderwebs, leaving only the pure polished reflecting walls of the mind, lucidity.

in the next section the line-series returns upon itself, spirals, and even is momentarily fixed circularly in a four-polar symmetry, which we saw was implied in the crude *Ancienne Étude*, i.e., the unity and duality phases are compressed into a unity-duality paradox and, since the sameness-difference of the paradox is itself paradoxical, a paradox of paradox, a tetrapolarity, is set up. Mallarmé calls this momentary result a *symétrie parfaite*. Since even in this more static circular system (as opposed to the linear) a regress is operative—paradox, paradox of paradox, etc., ad infinitum—the success is again only temporary: a movement is made towards polypolarity, but the mind falters at this level of (conscious) speculation and with it the text.[39]

The circular regress (tetrapolarity) is already begun in *Le Minuit*: the light-dark duality (become polarity) is crossed by a time-polarity, present-past.

In the second section (*Il quitte la chambre et se perd dans les escaliers*), here is the linear regress again:

> une douteuse perception de pendule [DUALITY] qui va s'atteindre et expirer en lui [Igitur: UNITY]; mais à ce qui luit et va, expirant en soi, s'éteindre, elle se voit qui le porte encore [DUALITY] . . . le bruit total et dénué à jamais tomba en son passé [UNITY]. (p. 436)

Now circular regress begins again:

> D'un côté si l'équivoque [DUALITY become polarity] cessa [UNITY] une motion de l'autre, dure [l'un côté versus l'autre = polarity of polarity], marquée plus pressante par un double heurt . . . et dont un frôlement

39. One can consider tetrapolarity to be the deepest penetration, for practical purposes, of Mallarmé into his own mind. Concretized as the "symphonic equation," it constitutes the armature of the *Coup de Dés*: a vibration that vibrates in the white spaces separating the four phases of the title phrase.

> actuel . . . remplit confusément l'équivoque ou sa ces-
> sation: comme si la chute totale qui avait été le choc
> unique des portes du tombeau, n'en étouffait pas l'hôte
> sans retour. . . . (p. 436)

Here the first duality, *équivoque*, is cancelled (*cessa*),
and from amid this vibration of unity-duality another
vibration arises, crossing it (*remplit confusément*) at
right angles, i.e., the polarity is polarized. The *portes
du tombeau* is a concretization of the first polarity or
équivoque and is clearly indicated in several fragments
as a paradox of two panels both opened and closed "à
la fois ouverts et fermés" (p. 450); the sound of the
choc of the closed doors (canceled duality) remains—
just as the *Clarté* remained in the previous section—as an
asymmetric element indicating that the victory is still
incomplete, and this element is the first pole of the new
duality crossing the initial one. This new duality, a new
équivoque, is now called (p. 436) "l'incertitude issue
probablement de la tournure affirmative" (i.e., the asymmetric result, cf. *choc*) and in it

> se présente une vision de la chute interrompue de pan-
> neaux, comme si c'était soi-même qui, doué du mouve-
> ment suspendu, le retournât sur soi en la spirale ver-
> tigineuse conséquente. . . . (p. 437)

i.e., the canceled duality of *panneaux* plunged the mind
into neutrality-darkness, but the consciousness of this
result remains (victory is defeat) and forms with the
neutrality-darkness the second polarity, *chute interrompue*: the *choc* or *mouvement suspendu* thus seems to pop
up from the dark in a movement reversing the cancella-
tion-plunge. This *returning* movement is the obvious
beginning of a spiral, for each downward movement
circles back on itself, "retourne sur soi" ("comme si
c'était soi-même qui, doué du mouvement suspendu, le

retournât sur soi," p. 437), and the series of movements creates the linearity of a spiral that "devait être indéfiniment fuyante." Here we have reached the intermediate spiral stage (not yet the more perfectly circular *symétrie parfaite* of tetrapolarity):

> la spirale . . . devait être indéfiniment fuyante, si une oppression progressive, poids graduel de ce dont on ne se rendait pas compte, malgré que ce fût expliqué en somme, n'en eût impliqué l'évasion certaine en un intervalle, la cessation; où, lorsqu'expira le heurt, et qu'elles [*l'oppression* et *l'évasion*] se confondirent, rien en effet ne fut plus ouï que le battement d'ailes absurdes de quelque hôte effrayé de la nuit heurté dans son lourd somme par la clarté et prolongeant sa fuite indéfinie.
> (p. 437)

Here the spiral or infinite regress is totally interrupted and reversed; the mind returns in a resolving "leap," from a thought-regress back to the level of concrete reality: the *oppression progressive* was the increasing faltering of the mind down at the unbreathable level of paradox (and paradox of paradox, etc.), and there is a natural rebellion of the system *effrayé* (life asserting itself ultimately as self-preserving impulse; cf. the total "kinetic excess" mentioned in my syntax chapter of *L'Oeuvre de Mallarmé*); the attempt to get beyond the vibration-spiral of *chute interrompue*, to explain it ("expliqué en somme," p. 437) is canceled, not beyond but on this side, in a return to normal reality. This defeat is the *évasion*, and the *cessation* is an arational (concrete) cancellation: thus the spiral, which was thought-movement "underneath," has become concretized as a frightened bird, later recognized as the frightened beating heart. Igitur, however, does not accept this as a defeat since he himself, in a new effort, realizes the nature of the case and, dismissing contemptuously the *quelque hôte effrayé* as being aroused directly because of the power of his conception ("heurté dans son lourd somme par la clarté," p. 437), he prepares a new *résumé* of the case that, when it is fully understood as a symmetry, will constitute success.

In the next paragraph the heartbeat is seen as a necessary precondition of the deed; it symbolizes the body-site against which the perfect attempt will be pitted, or the past of ancestors against which the perfect present will be realized:

> pour que l'ombre dernière se mirât en son propre soi [i.e., the past has to be accepted, taken up into the symmetry just as *hasard*-negation had to be accepted —or "absorbed" as he says later], et se reconnût en la foule de ses apparitions . . . telles, à présent, se voyant pour qu'elle se voie, elle, pure, l'Ombre, ayant sa dernière forme qu'elle foule, derrière elle. (p. 437)

The new acceptance is a new victory, *derrière elle*, Igitur being canceled together with his ancestors; this constitutes the unity of "pure, l'Ombre" (cf. the previous "Chaos, de l'ombre").

This present-past polarity can be conceived as a further development beyond the tetrapolarity of the preceding section towards polypolarity, but because of the intervening failure (total "resolving" return to concreteness) I take it, as in all such cases, as a new start[40] (except in one instance of the *Touches* [W], where a vertical dimension is tentatively added, creating a polypolarity). Thus the new polarity forms, together with a new polarity of light-dark (concretized again as the candle and

40. The conscious mind can handle only a tetrapolarity successfully: most people never get that far but falter at the first unidimensional paradox.

the book), a new tetrapolarity. The past-present polarity is extended to a past-future one and vibrates in a paradox so that past and future are canceled and simultaneous:

l'étendue de couches[41] d'ombre, rendue à la nuit pure, de toutes ses nuits pareilles apparues, des couches à jamais séparées d'elles et que sans doute elles ne connurent pas (p. 437)

i.e., the duality of past-future is momentarily seen as a multiplicity or series of light and dark alternations: (a) a series of ancestor-shadows; (b) (later more clearly) the infinite series of reflections of Igitur in the shining opposing walls of the room, which series splits clearly into a tetrapolarity in the four shining walls,[42] so that the reflection-series is itself reflected:

des deux côtés les myriades d'ombres pareilles, et de leurs deux côtés, dans les parois opposés, qui se réfléchissaient ... l'inverse de ces ombres ... ombre négative d'eux-mêmes [the *côtés*]: c'était le lieu de la certitude parfaite.... (p. 446)

and (c) (later) a series of black ancestral shadows separated by their white tombstones (like milestones of history), etc. The "à jamais séparées d'elles" means that the series has been canceled so that, as Igitur stands in the static darkness, the remembered black nights are equally in front of him (future and past are one) and thus estranged from their former separate or multiple selves. Only in Igitur will the multiple shadows become the single shadow that will know itself.

41. "Les mots ... gisent ... de dates diverses comme des stratifications: vite je parlerai de couches" (p. 901).

42. Note in passing that an early posthumously published *Cahier* (written at age seventeen) was entitled *Entre quatre murs* (Gallimard, 1954).

The final phrase "qui n'est, je le sais, que le prolongement absurde du bruit de la fermeture de la porte sépulcrale dont l'entrée de ce puits rappelle la porte" (p. 437)
goes back to the *soupçon* (before the long phrase separated by two dashes from the rest of the paragraph),
and this *soupçon* is exactly like the *Clarté*, an asymmetry
or imperfection: this first phrase merely repeats an exactly similar earlier one we have discussed. The *puits*
is a new concretization of the cancellation, this time seen
as in the future, *devant*.

The next passage reads:

> Cette fois, plus nul doute; la certitude se mire en
> l'évidence: en vain, réminiscence d'un mensonge, dont
> elle était la conséquence, la vision d'un lieu apparaissait-
> elle encore, telle que devait être, par exemple, l'inter-
> valle attendu, ayant, en effet, pour parois latérales l'op-
> position double des panneaux, et pour vis-à-vis, devant
> et derrière, l'ouverture de doute nul, répercutée par le
> prolongement du bruit des panneaux, où s'enfuit le
> plumage, et dédoublée par l'équivoque exploré, la sym-
> étrie parfaite des déductions prévues démentait sa ré-
> alité; il n'y avait pas à s'y tromper c'était la conscience
> de soi (à laquelle l'absurde même devait servir de lieu)
> —sa réussite. (pp. 437–38)

Here we have reached the peak of Igitur's effort via the
absurde, i.e., paradox. In a final attempt to put a halt
to the regress he has violently compressed the last-
generated opposites by accepting a kind of compromise
of madness (later *folie utile*), i.e., the last consciousness
of the symmetry must be at the same time unconscious
(willed-unwilled), and this is the *absurde* or the *mensonge* (phenomenon as fiction), and the *réalité démen-
tie*. In retrospect he considers the paradox of time future
and time past as also absurd, and therefore his present
conception is a "réminiscence d'un mensonge": the

present conception he considers as only temporary (it will be eclipsed by the *folie* or *absurde*) and negligible (not destructive of his symmetry) since he had foreseen it; therefore it is an "intervalle attendu," and in any case it too is symmetric, for it is a tetrapolarity with the original *panneaux* as the first pair of contrasts and, as second polarity, the frightening *choc* of their closing versus the comprehension of that fright as a necessary precondition (see preceding paragraph: the ancestors). This new summing-up of the tetrapolarity, being moreover a going-over again of the tetrapolarity of the preceding section and thus creating another rudimentary symmetry (which is really a mere repetition and therefore negligible) satisfies him, provisionally, as a success: the *absurde* raised to the second power [a spatial absurdity of light-dark (or *panneaux* both opened and closed) crossed by a temporal absurdity of past-future (or doubt-no doubt)] is the "conscience de soi"[43] and an exact parallel, as I note elsewhere ("Syntax," in *L'Oeuvre de Mallarmé*) of Kierkegaard's "absolute paradox" (in *Riens philosophiques*).

Here, finally, is another particularly lucid example of the pattern:

> Ce qu'il y avait de clair c'est que ce séjour concordait parfaitement avec lui-même: des deux côtés les myriades d'ombres pareilles, et de leurs deux côtés, dans les parois opposées, qui se réfléchissaient, deux trouées d'ombre massive qui devait être nécessairement l'inverse de ces ombres, non leur apparition, mais leur disparition, ombre négative d'eux-mêmes: c'était le lieu de la certitude parfaite. (p. 446)

43. "Ma Pensée s'est pensée" (letter to Cazalis, 14 May 1867); this is a complete correspondence of self as subject and object; cf. Spinoza's "intellectual love of God" (or the perfectly "adequate").

II

Text and Detailed Commentary

Igitur ou la folie d'Elbehnon

Ce conte s'adresse à l'intelligence du lecteur qui met les choses
en scène, elle-même.

S. M.

THE NAME of the hero, Igitur, and of his ancestral manorial site have been discussed in previous pages; in essence, they bear hints of what he does, his dramatic act
—*folie*—as we saw. Actor, scene, and act are accordingly
in the interpenetrating sort of relationship that we expect of poetic art, especially symbolist art.

In certain fragments of his project for a *Grand
Oeuvre* (which Bonniot arbitrarily published together
with his early edition of *Igitur*), Mallarmé explored
these relationships in the terms of "polypolarity." Here
the three entities—actor, scene, act—are called *Héros*,
Théâtre, and *Drame*. In triadic Hegelian terms, drama
can be seen as the synthesis of hero (thesis) and theater
(antithesis). These poles of reality are in a complex
dialectical relationship already in Hegel, but Mallarmé
needed something even more complex and fluid: "Le
Drame est en le mystère / de l'équation suivante / que
théâtre / est / le développement du héros ou héros / le
résumé du théâtre / comme Idée et hymne / d'où Théâtre = idée / héros = hymne / et cela forme un tout /

59

Drame ou Mystère / rentrant l'un en l'autre / aussi" (p. 429).

This formula is also presented in the accompanying scheme. This is clearly what we call a tetrapolarity: the

Théâtre	Idée

Myst[ère]
↓
Dr[ame]

Héros	Hymne
(mime)	(danse)

four poles are *Théâtre*, *Héros*, *Idée*, *Hymne*, with *Drame* (or *Mystère*) as the nodal point ("quintessential" as we call it in this tetrapolar case).

If we arbitrarily say *Théâtre* is positive, *Héros*, negative, and *Idée*, positive, *Hymne*, negative, we have a typical tetrapolar situation in which two polarities are set up—two "dimensions"—that are soon seen to be equivalent and interchangeable. That is what Mallarmé is saying in the above notes, i.e., the apparently fragmentary hero emerges from the total ("positive") site —which is eventually the cosmos—as the hymn emerges from the total idea. Yet a hero has deep metaphysical personality, is as profoundly rooted in the cosmos as the site—in an obvious old form-matter (or trace-presence) dilemma—and so the two poles are reversible. The same is true for *Idée* and *Hymne*: the expression that molds the idea is like its little person, or hero. So all that forms "un tout" as Mallarmé says. Or elsewhere on the margin:

[équation]   faite d'une double
                    identité
             équation ou idée
             si ceci est cela
             cela est ceci

Note that the *Drame-Mystère* polarity merely extends the tetrapolarity to a tentative hexapolar scheme, but that is not important for our purposes. More interesting is the fact that we can go a step or two farther than Mallarmé did in these sketchy notes and see that a more complete epistemological investigation would proceed along the following lines.

Théâtre = a horizontal dimension, objective, total, with *héros* = the vertical, subjective, fragmentary. But these, as we saw, are immediately reversible. The same is true of *Idée* and *Hymne*. We then, in a new frame of reference, put these four terms, as poles, into a tetrapolar relationship, as Mallarmé did, but noting that initially *Idée* and *Hymne*, being more objective, should form the horizontal polarity, *Théâtre-Héros*, the vertical. But then these two dimensions are seen as reversible . . .

The little words *mime* and *danse* in the scheme above are merely the expressive media of the fragmentary "molding" figures, the hero or the hymn, extending, as it were, the idea of expression but at the same time spiraling back to an objectivity (a dance is an objective act, etc.)[1] so that the interpenetrating paradoxical aspect of the formula is emphasized.

Going back to the title: Elbehnon is the "theater," summing up the whole cosmic site as always in Mallarmé's meditations on the theater—thus the room of Igitur will "blow up" or open to the sea-sky totality, in suggestion at least—and we can initially imagine it as horizontal like the earth site of mankind or a stage. Igitur is the hero—vertical, subjective. But the reversibility is evident in the fact that the actor creates the site by looking at it. And the hero then becomes the objec-

1. As Yeats emphasizes in *Among School Children*, Valéry in "L'Ame et la danse."

tive totality from whom emerge partial "scenes." The drama is his act—*folie*—summing up the interplay between these two dimensions, at the nodal point, as it were, but adding that an act implies a departure from a static "cross" into a diachronic spiral, entering on-going time as movement, like the wave movement emerging from the primal constellatory tensions of the *Coup de Dés*. In other words, act too is polar, paradoxical, and begins a third dimension of polypolarity as *Drame-Mystère* did (indeed, *Mystère* can be seen as a more open, vibrant, moving form of drama as well as the reverse).

As profoundly true as all this is, one is perhaps a bit relieved to emerge from the epistemological whirl into the "prevailing forms" that characterize life as we ordinarily think of and live it. Here a theater is unquestionably a site, a hero unquestionably a strutting erect person, at least for a while. And his act emerges unequivocally from him, as a gesture of his arm: the dice throw, a child of his personality as he is a child of his environment (corresponding to the *mime*, above). But when we rethink the matter, alas, we rediscover that the act or *mime*—*folie*—is an ancestor, not just a "child" or product, and predates the whole business as an "absurdity" from the beginning. This is what Mallarmé means by the concise passage (cited earlier) about *hasard* always having its way. Or as Valéry put it, "au commencement était la blague."

The little epigraph is in line with what we have just said: the *scène* (of "*en scène*") is the total metaphysical site, hence beyond any partial, local scene; it is located in the "intelligence" in that sense. Mallarmé always returned to this total drama, always eventually was dissatisfied with the limitations of the theater of his time whenever he thought of working with it. The fireplace, as in "Crayonné au théâtre," became, at times, that comprehensive inner theater . . .

The mixture of genres implied in this is characteristic of Mallarmé in the same sense of back to the source where everything almost converges, not only genres but all the different arts. This results in his meditations in which he modifies the *Gesamtkunstwerk* of Wagner into something more inner, less heteroclite, flamboyant, and extrovert. In poetry, such as the *Coup de Dés*, there is drama (dramatic action), music (well, verbal music), visual effects, and even a sort of ballet of type. He explores the common roots of music and letters in the essay of that name and the near-convergence of the other arts *passim*; note that I say *near*-convergence, as in my earlier observations on Mallarmé's poetic universe (*O.*, pp. 81, 401).

Epistemologically, we can see the relation between the arts and genres as follows.

Music is the vertical, holistic (circular, fluid, metaphoric, implying communion); letters are the horizontal, fragmentary (linear or ad hoc, articulated, metonymic, implying communication). This is an initial view, which is arbitrary, to be sure, since, as in the case of theater, we could have seen music as objectivity on a horizontal dimension; but the initial scheme is familiar today and is just as workable as another one. Painting is another dimension, related to music as letters are—if we think of drawn alphabet characters, writing—in one way, although we can obviously see painting as simple and total. Does sight precede sound? All the senses are supposed to emerge biologically from one main trunk, feeling. Perhaps since we cannot close our ears and we articulate our eyes—blink—we can understand hearing as being more primordial, as Vico and Joyce did, starting reality with a thunderclap, corresponding to what they take the first impression of life to be to a new-born child, a "big bang" of a sort as he emerges from the womb and a rush of air hits his eardrums. But there are sound waves—rhythms—and the ear has an articulating apparatus corresponding to that rhythmic movement (see Derrida, "Le tympan"). So we seem to have a standoff here and are forced to settle for an arbitrary order: painting (or music), then letters. And, as Derrida insists, in opposition to Rousseau and others, since letters —*la trace*—are just as prior, we have another version of the chicken-and-egg situation, which we really never left.

But, in order to keep some sense of direction, let's say again: painting-music-letters. Within letters, one is inclined to put poetry first, as more total or whole (Vico, Hugo, and Joyce concur on this), more artistic in that sense, and prose in the metonymic fragmentary position, horizontal. Or if we think of drama as poetry, then dramatic poetry second (since it involves acts, which are linear, etc.), prose third. But drama, we noted along with Mallarmé, can mean the nodal point and be prior. The circle is still with us, obviously, and with it the reason for the near-convergence of the genres when we get this metaphysical. Hence Mallarmé can call his piece a *conte* and yet imply it is a drama and it can also be, as it clearly is, poetry in some meaningful sense.[2]

(A)

ANCIENNE ÉTUDE
Quand les souffles de ses ancêtres veulent
souffler la bougie, (grâce à laquelle peut-être

2. See *Modes of Art*, chapter 6.

subsistent les caractères du grimoire)—il dit
« Pas encore! »

Lui-même à la fin, quand les bruits auront
disparu, tirera une preuve de quelque chose
de grand (pas d'astres? le hasard annulé?) de
ce simple fait qu'il peut causer l'ombre en
soufflant sur la lumière—

Puis—comme il aura parlé selon l'absolu
—qui nie l'immortalité, l'absolu existera en
dehors—lune, au-dessus du temps: et il soulèvera les rideaux, en face.

Igitur, tout enfant, lit son devoir à ses ancêtres.

This is a tentative outline of the whole *conte*. Here,
the diachronic precedes the static drama (synchronic).
There is no initial moment of resolve here: only those
two phases.

Quand les souffles: A spirit from the beginning of
time[3] comes down through Igitur's racial ancestry, seeking to act through him, an act predicted—as we soon
learn—in the magic book (*grimoire*) mentioned here.
Note that *souffle* is linked with spirit traditionally, as in
Hebrew *Ruach*; Latin *anima*; *âme*, etc. The implication
is that before Igitur, the wish of the *ancêtres*—to blow
out the candle, as in *Macbeth*—is not ripe, neither
sounded sufficiently in depth, instinctively, nor made
sufficiently conscious. Igitur wants to be fully aware of
his act, responsible for his consciousness and its annihila-
tion—psychic suicide—symbolized in the blowing out of
the candle in order to achieve a purity, the absolute.

3. Cf. the "ancestralement . . . ultérieur démon immémorial"
of Page 5 of the *Coup de Dés*.

Later, in the *conte*, the possibility of an actual suicide is contemplated, as in *Hamlet*, involving poison. One thinks of the Gospels ("lose all to gain all"), of the German Romantic philosophers Stirner and Hartmann, of Dostoevsky's Kirilov, and, in terms of psychic suicide, of the "absurdists," such as Kierkegaard and Berdiyaev, as discussed by Camus in *Le Mythe de Sisyphe*.

ancêtres: In Alfred de Vigny's *l'Esprit pur*—Jacques Gengoux originally drew my attention to it—the poet brags that he has illustrated his line, adding a "plume de fer qui n'est pas sans beauté" to the ancestral helmet, which is related to the ambiguous *plume* of the writer, etc., of the *Coup de Dés*: "J'ai fait illustre un nom qu'on m'a transmis sans gloire"; cf. the "ancestralement à n'ouvrir pas la main" of the *Coup de Dés*, Page 5. Moreover: "Dans le caveau des miens plongeant mes pas nocturnes, / J'ai compté mes aïeux, suivant leur vieille loi. / J'ouvris leurs parchemins. . ." very likely had some effect on the nocturnal, tomblike chamber of *Igitur* and his descent into the ancestral vault, plus the *grimoire* that descended from the past, and so on. Vigny goes on: "A peine une étincelle a relui dans leur cendre"; that too corresponds to the *antique idée* (I, G) of Igitur, the mere spark he got from the *ancêtres*, which he will vivify, thus becoming in a sense their father, their presiding spirit: "Ils descendront de moi." See under *tout enfant* below.

Les caractères du grimoire: for Mallarmé, in many a text, they carry all the meaning of the cosmos in their mystery; a *caractère* is a homunculus, a microcosmic figure, like the little Hamlet figure of the letter *i* on Page 8 of the *Coup de Dés* (*O.*, pp. 89–97). "In the beginning was the word"; but as I note in my *Oeuvre de Mallarmé*

66

(*O.*, pp. 31, 236, etc.), the poet was constantly aware of the chicken-and-egg paradox and becoming-spiral involving light and dark, totality and fragment (expression), form (*trace*) and matter, male and female, all implied in the dialectic of the character, on the white or blank page (see p. 370 especially), as in the extended dialectic of the candle (light) and dark sign.

grimoire: a "gramarye," or "magic book," "black book," etc., in occult tradition. The term is found on page 292 of the *Dogme et rituel de la haute magie*, by Eliphas Lévi, which Villiers had recommended to Mallarmé in 1867 (the alchemical term *Grand Oeuvre*, which Mallarmé also uses, in reference to his Masterwork, is likewise found in this book, p. 259). Not that that proves Mallarmé read it or, in any case, that he was thoroughly influenced by it; in his *Notes*, for example, he takes pains to keep his distance from occultism, which, as he says, separates into a cult what belongs to a universal vision, literary in his case. But it is at least interesting that the concept of tetrapolarity occurs there, in chapter 4. We will return to this question in greater detail in chapter 4 of this study.

Mallarmé uses *grimoire* generically as *the* book, which comes down in time from the all-source; for example, in his *Hommage* (*à Wagner*): "notre si vieil ébat triomphal du grimoire." It is used very much in the sense of *Igitur*, i.e., an old book needing revivifying by the final heir of a tradition, in *Prose* (*pour des Esseintes*): "ma mémoire . . . aujourd'hui grimoire / Dans un livre de fer vêtu." The reason he likes the word is clearly the echo association with *mémoire* (a sort of mental text, in time, as in Hamlet's "fond trivial records"); also with *moire*, a cloth, because of the *textus* (woven) "text" connotation. Maybe too the element *grime*, "old man," or *grimer*, "to make up as an old man," contributes to the feeling of ancientness, cf. English *grim* and *grime*.[4]

In Keats' *Endymion*, Book III, there is a description of "mouldering scrolls / Writ in the tongue of heaven, by those souls / Who first were on the earth." It is linked with a drama of spiritual succession wherein a divine sage, an Old Man of the Sea, hands down his task to "A youth . . . whom he shall direct / How to consummate all." The shipwreck theme, the old Master, and much else has passed into the imagery of the *Coup de Dés*, as I demonstrated in "Keats and Mallarmé" (*Comp. Lit. Studies* 7, no. 2, pp. 195–203). It is hardly surprising to find suggestions of this relation in *Igitur*, though, again, nothing is proved. . . Cf. "père qui . . . avait préparé à fils . . . une tâche sublime" (*Pour un Tombeau d'Anatole*, ed. J.-P. Richard, Seuil, 1961, p. 106).

Pas encore!: Explained above; the old *souffle* is not yet ready, fully conscious. Mallarmé plays at times with the ambiguity of negative and positive in *pas* as "not" and "step" (*O.*, pp. 406, 644).

The polarity of light and characters starts the complex drama whose armature is a series of substitutions of that dialectic—or its complication into tetrapolar and even polypolar form—as we have noted earlier. The light-dark of candle-characters is in a metonymic dialectic chain of historical Becoming, or life as it is carried on unfinally, cf. the "hiéroglyphes dont s'exalte le millier" of the *Hommage* (*à Wagner*) or the "pli de sombre dentelle qui retient l'infini, tissé par mille" (p. 370). Igitur will face a total dialectic of light-dark in

4. Cf. the preface to *Vathek*, "Cette jeunesse . . . exilée d'entre les grimoires de la bibliothèque paternelle" (p. 551).

the candle versus the surrounding total *ombre*; cf. Wagner's *originel*, total art versus the *millier* in the *Hommage* to him.

The candle, book, and clock *sonnerie* may echo the traditional "bell, book, and candle" of magic ritual, but I suspect they are Mallarmé's spontaneously similar, inventive imagery.

Lui-même à la fin: one thinks of Mallarmé's "tel qu'en lui-même enfin" (*Tombeau d'Edgar Poe*); he enjoys the overtone of *lui* as "shone" as in the "météore, lui" of his essay on Rimbaud.

bruits: the candle is likely from *Macbeth*, which Mallarmé read early and commented on in an essay (p. 346). The celebrated lines, "Out, out, brief candle! / Life's but a walking shadow, a poor player / That struts and frets his hour upon the stage. . . . It is a tale / Told by an idiot, full of sound and fury, / Signifying nothing," may be also a source for the idea of sound as empty "noise" (*bruits*), or random vain life "outside" or before him. Certainly the whole sequence impressed Mallarmé deeply with its "nothing." The various *bruits* later in the text, as parts of the inane *folie* of life as the ancestors lived it, are certainly implied here. There is later on an occasional indication of a theatrical setting in which Igitur plays before an ancestral public, which whistles (*siffler*); these are part of the *bruits* effect, the vanity of flux, the mere hum and buzz of trivial existence, versus his *absolu*.

The candle also may suggest the famous Cartesian meditation on wax, as Rottenberg suggests after Philippe Sollers, but that is less likely.

preuve: the fusion of light and dark, summed up in the melting of stars into their dark background—or the

corollary disappearance (cancellation) of number, symbolized by the stars, i.e., all the combinations of dice
throws of fate or Becoming, all emanated or dissem-
inated reality, as on Page 9 of the *Coup de Dés*, the
endless phenomena of Chance. This annulment would
result in a victory of the absolute, Igitur provisionally,
or questioningly, thinks here. Later he will see that this
victory is an asymmetry and will try to cancel it in a
more complex dialectic, symbolized by the four reflecting walls of the chamber of his mind.

Contrary to what previous critics have believed, it is
because Mallarmé will discover the infinite regress in
this that he will abandon his project; that endless whirl
of mentality will send him back to a human—though unprecedentedly deep—*jeu* without any finality other than
a far-out, glimpsed, or implied one.

pas d'astres? le hasard annulé?: the fusion of opposites
variously is thought of as the stars melting into the dark
night background, as the blowing out of the candle, or
as the dots on the dice cube, like the characters of the
book, similarly disappearing; cf. "hasard absorbé" (T).

soufflant: this spirit-breath is conceived as another
fusion of a physical gesture and a mental one, as in the
"souffle de ton nom" of the *Sonnet pour votre chère
morte* or the "agitation solennelle par l'air / De paroles"
and the "frisson final, dans sa voix seule" of *Toast
funèbre*. Thus the "parlé selon l'absolu" below.

immortalité: the full acceptance of chance (madness,
etc.) in an absurdist psychic death, a baptismal maneuver à la St. Jean but without the Christian hope of
afterlife, a death-rebirth somehow in *this* life, like Kir-

ilov's in Dostoevsky's *Possessed* or Nietzsche's "Eternal Return."

The denial of any sentimental belief in immortality is existential in flavor: Kierkegaard's refusal of Hegel's "panlogical" dialectic in favor of the stark "either-or" is the crucial example, followed by Heidegger's *Sein zum Tode*: death is. This is the mood of Mallarmé's pagan *Toast funèbre*, his homage to the lucidly stoic Gautier, where he refuses the "magique espoir du corridor" and imagines cosmic catastrophe: *soleil mortel.*

l'absolu existera en dehors: an objectivity arising with the self-cancellation of his act. It will remain like the objective perfection of *en-soi* and *pour-soi* combined that Sartre sees as everyman's vain hope, at the end of *L'Être et le Néant*, or the aim to be God without ceasing to be a man, which was Malraux's equivalent, in *La Condition humaine*. But Mallarmé, like other artistic souls, thought it possible at times: "Je suis maintenant impersonnel . . . une aptitude qu'a l'Univers spirituel à se voir" (letter to Cazalis, 14 May 1867, *Corr.*, p. 242). Cf. Nietzsche's "obedience," Rilke's "poem-objects," Archibald MacLeish's definition of poetry as not meaning but being, Heidegger's *Geworfenheit*. Camus' equivalent of the moon of Mallarmé is a rock, in the *Mythe de Sisyphe*; cf. *La Halte à Oran* ("Oh to be nothing . . . like a rock") or *La Pierre qui pousse*.

lune: its placid roundness is part of its *it*ness, its self-sufficiency. There *it* is like the universe after our departure in the *Coup de Dés*, Pages 10 and 11; we are mere visitors, inessential.

Mallarmé didn't always see the moon that way. It seemed compromised by a sentimental half-light in the

71

Romantic tradition, and he called it a "cheese" in a letter to Coppée, dreamed of dissolving it and leaving the eternal drama to the "pur soleil mortel" (*Toast funèbre*).

au-dessus du temps: human, chronological, and linear time will have given way to a static, circular concept, *hors du temps*, as in Proust; Einstein's closed space-time universe is a corollary concept.

il soulèvera les rideaux: that gesture is the self-effacement before the objective outdoors, the cosmos (with its inhuman moon); it is somewhat theatrical in overtone and is linked perhaps to the feminine duality of tomb-womb panels later. These curtains open onto the all-womb, cf. the Ark, the total mystery. The "temps de la chambre vide . . . jusqu'à ce qu'on l'ouvre [la fenêtre]" (p. 135) of *Pour un Tombeau d'Anatole* is comparable: a pagan yielding to the eternity of nature of which Mallarmé's son is still in some sense a part. But in *Une dentelle s'abolit* the creativity of nature in this sense is most dubious; at least until the end of the sonnet, maybe . . .

tout enfant: this evocation of the original and *originel*, harking back to Igitur as "a small child," will be developed in the *Vie d'Igitur*. His own childhood haunts him, as does Hamlet's, "l'adolescent évanoui de nous aux commencements de la vie . . . personnage unique d'une tragédie intime et occulte" ("Hamlet," p. 299). In the term "juvénile fantôme" (p. 299), the echo *enfant-fantôme* is important here, as it will be on Page 5 of the *Coup de Dés*. As in that cosmic and evolutionary text, Igitur is also a child in the sense of "child of his race" —"fils de l'homme"—vis-à-vis the *ancêtres* below, and a child of nature, ingenuous, pure as the Faun, a Hamlet child standing before the cosmos like the *flanc enfant* of the drowned *sirène* of *À la nue accablante tu*. Hamlet, his model, was often infantine—particularly at his mother's feet—in his *folie* or recalled his childhood, as in the graveyard scene. The reminiscence of Igitur's own youth, appropriate to his fateful cyclic moment, is brought out strongly in fragment AC.

Tout enfant has an overtone of "everychild"; just as Mallarmé thought of Hamlet's Passion as that of everyman, "l'Homme."

lit son devoir: he is like a child rehearsing his lessons to grown-ups as he addresses his ancestors. This could be also, ambiguously, his act conceived as a duty handed down over the years, cf. the *devoir idéal* descended from ancestral poets or nature in *Toast funèbre*. There is an implication also that he shows their duty to them, as in Vigny's *L'Esprit pur*: "ils descendront de moi."

These tentative notations for the *Vie d'Igitur* are not only a part of his past history, but the basis for a cyclic recurrence or "arrestation," as in certain of the later fragments (e.g., AD), where he does act in a clearly infantile way.

(B)

4 MORCEAUX:

1. *Le Minuit*
2. *L'Escalier*
3. *Le Coup de dés*
4. *Le Sommeil sur les cendres,
   après la bougie soufflée*

These four phases of the drama correspond roughly to the four seasons of the "symphonique équation propre aux saisons" (p. 646), which Mallarmé announced as the armature of the *Grand Oeuvre* and which were

embodied in the four phases of the title phrase: UN
COUP DE DÉS / JAMAIS / N'ABOLIRA / LE HASARD, as I
discuss them in my *Oeuvre de Mallarmé* (*O.*, pp. 53–60).

1. Le Minuit: a diamond-bright high point of the
mind corresponding to summer or high noon (on the
clock face, with its four cardinal points of noon or midnight, three, six, nine). It is the vibrant moment of end
and beginning of the cycle of universes in total time, the
brilliant star or sun flash (Big Bang) that begins the new
cosmogonic evolution. Thus UN COUP DE DÉS was placed
high up on the initial page.

2. L'Escalier: a median, transitional moment of descent corresponding to three o'clock and fall; cf. JAMAIS,
at mid-page.

3. Le Coup de dés: down in the tomb, the vertically
extreme, low moment of psychic death, corresponding
to winter (N'ABOLIRA, at the bottom of a page).

4. Le Sommeil sur les cendres, après la bougie soufflée:
another median, or transitional, moment, corresponding
to spring (cf. LE HASARD, neutral, at midpoint of the
near-final page). At this point, Igitur is awaiting the result, obviously, of his *coup*, a hoped-for earthly re-
awakening.

We do not know the order in which Mallarmé composed these fragments, but it seems likely that this one
was a later, more definitive approach to the armature
of his subject than the others, since it is in the pattern
of the fully realized and later *Coup de Dés*.

(C)

A PEU PRÈS CE QUI SUIT:

Minuit sonne—le Minuit où doivent être
jetés les dés. Igitur descend les escaliers, de

l'esprit humain, va au fond des choses: en
« absolu » qu'il est. Tombeaux—cendres (pas
sentiment, ni esprit), neutralité. Il récite la
prédiction et fait le geste. Indifférence. Sifflements dans l'escalier. « Vous avez tort »
nulle émotion. L'infini sort du hasard, que
vous avez nié. Vous, mathématiciens expirâtes—moi projeté absolu. Devais finir en Infini. Simplement parole et geste. Quant à ce
que je vous dis, pour expliquer ma vie. Rien
ne restera de vous—L'infini enfin échappe à
la famille, qui en a souffert,—vieil espace—pas
de hasard. Elle a eu raison de le nier,—sa vie
—pour qu'il ait été l'absolu. Ceci devait avoir
lieu dans les combinaisons de l'Infini vis-à-vis
de l'Absolu. Nécessaire—extrait l'Idée. Folie
utile. Un des actes de l'univers vient d'être
commis là. Plus rien, restait le souffle, fin de
parole et geste unis—souffle la bougie de
l'être, par quoi tout a été. Preuve.

(Creuser tout cela)

This passage goes with the preceding one (B) and is
part of the same outline sketch.

Minuit sonne—le Minuit où doivent être jetés les dés:
This has been discussed previously. It is the end-of-
cycle point when worlds are born; the point of "baptismal" return to origin, spirally, in a psychic death-rebirth.
There are numerous equivalents in mystic tradition,
some of which will be treated in our final section (chapter 4); an obvious example from familiar folklore is the
magic midnight of the New Year, with its symbolism
of old man and (mysteriously related) babe.

The closest parallel is Mallarmé's "Sonnet en yx"—*Ses purs ongles*—originally written in 1866. There is a comparable confrontation between a protagonist of all time (*le Maître*) and fate; the Master has performed his suicidal act and disappeared, leaving the dark empty room with a mirror, as in *Igitur*, with the reflected pure stars—joining the macro of nature to the micro of the interior—as his legacy, symbolizing an objective Great Work, the coldly superior "It," a constellation of artistic strokes by Olympian genius. The moment of the drama is precisely, as here, a *Minuit*.

Mallarmé noted in "Crise de vers" the "perversity" that put bright letters (*i, u*) in a dark word *nuit* (or dark *ou* in *jour*). But he further noted that the loss in the material of language was created poetry's gain; the poet takes these ambiguities into account, or reinforces for certain clear effects (as in the theories of Whorf). So here, the paradox of black night and bright moment, flash of mind—as in the *foudre* of illumination that occurs at the (black) death of St. John (*N.*, p. 203) is well served by his poetic awareness. That intense Midnight point of crystalline clarity is referred to later in reference to the *diamant*: "le rêve pur d'un Minuit . . . dont la Clarté" and "le feu pur du diamant de l'horloge" (G), which is like the intimate essence of this midnight illumination. In the *Sonnet* (*pour votre chère morte*) a life-and-death struggle of the soul occurs at a Midnight, as it does in Poe's *Raven* (translated by Mallarmé).

sonne: he will play later with the bright gleam in the associations *son or sonore* (from the root of *sonner*). (See *O.*, p. 120).

jetés les dés: three bright *é* sounds are effective poetically here.

escaliers de l'esprit humain: the generally spiral shape of stairs reflecting the human psychic and physical intestinal structure (and poetic or mystic tradition, including Dante's spiral descent into hell and equivalents in Rabelais and Piranesi) gave us organic imagery like that in Hugo's *Les Djinns*:

> Fuyons sous la spirale
> De l'escalier profond!
> Déjà s'éteint ma lampe,
> Et l'ombre de la rampe,
> Qui le long du mur rampe,
> Monte jusqu'au plafond.

or closer still, Baudelaire's:

> Un damné descendant sans lampe,
> Au bord d'un gouffre dont l'odeur
> Trahit l'humide profondeur,
> D'éternels escaliers sans rampe,
> Où veillent des monstres visqueux. . . .
> > (*L'Irrémédiable*)

Other possible sources will be presented in chapter 4.

va . . . est: clear from preceding discussion.

Tombeaux—cendres: the negative extreme—death, ashes—and the neutral are paradoxically related, as we observed earlier, as in the concepts of death and nothingness, cf. "indifféremment LE HASARD" of the *Coup de Dés*, Page 9, which is both the eternal defeat and the eternal neutrality, cf. the *Rien* of Page 10. These are the dead points where a new life-cycle (or Life) can begin.

Il récite: The *prédiction* is the verbal statement of his enterprise, handed down in the *grimoire*: "Un Coup de dés qui accomplit une prédiction, d'où a dépendu la vie d'une race" (IV, S). This spark from the past will, with

Igitur, give life to the race finally; ambiguously, their (ordinary) life depended on *not* fulfilling it. The *geste* (of self-annihilation) is the physical aspect of it. The two aspects will then finally be fused in the one *souffle*, see below.

Indifférence: his, versus the sentimentality of the public of ancestors who are stirred, probably in his own frightened breast, which prolongs them in a sense, genetically, i.e., as a part of himself he refuses.

Sifflements: the ancestors hiss their disapproval. How? In his imagination, in the vestigial stirring of his heart (confirmed in a later passage) or, as Claudel suggests, in the sound of gas jets along the stairs; it is true that Mallarmé associated gaslight with a vulgar public (*T.P.*, p. 161). And as is shown by the indication "Scène de Théâtre, ancien Igitur" (IV, S), Mallarmé had in mind—as he often did with his projects, always eventually abandoning the idea as too extroverted—a play version (cf. the *en scène* of the epigraph). Note that the polarity of "comédien" (IV, S) and audience is the spatial equivalent of heir-ancestors. And in this later passage, he will say "Ne sifflez pas, aux vents, aux ombres —si je compte, comédien [note this], jouer le tour—les 12—pas de hasard dans aucun sens."

The wind of *Toast funèbre* plays this same role of vain externality, "le vent des mots . . . pas dits," by non-poets, cf. the project of Mallarmé mentioned by George Moore in his *Avowals*, involving an Igiturlike figure living in a castle. The wind outside howls *ou-ou* emptily. If it rises in sound, becoming *oui*, he will go out, act. The *ou* of *souffle* and *doute* carry this phonostylistic impact.

L'infini sort: their sentimental refusal of the absurd-ity—chance—of existence denied them the converse *infini*, as the absolute (i.e., not infinite chance but infinite meaning). That is why just below he says "moi projeté absolu. Devais finir en Infini." The capital on *Infini* probably indicates a victory, a definitive form of infinite, associated with the absolute. It is also possible that he means "the infinite arises from, or resides in the heart of, chance (paradox), which you ancestors sentimentally denied." It comes to much the same thing.

Vous, mathématiciens: science in the old logical and nonabsurd sense failed as it had for Baudelaire: "Un de ces raisonneurs si communs, incapables de s'élever jusqu'à la logique de l'Absurde" (*Les Dons des fées*). Mallarmé recalls Descartes in his *Notes*, where he speaks of his own "langage mathématique" (p. 851) and projects his own new science based on the absurd: "La fiction lui semble être le procédé même de l'esprit" (p. 861). At first he evokes Descartes in terms of style. He then goes on as follows:

> Nous n'avons pas compris Descartes, l'étranger s'est emparé de lui: mais il a suscité les mathématiciens français.
>
> Il faut reprendre son mouvement, étudier nos mathématiciens—et ne nous servir de l'étranger, l'Allemagne ou l'Angleterre, que comme d'une contre-épreuve: nous aidant ainsi de ce qu'il [*l'étranger*] nous a pris.
>
> Du reste le mouvement hyper-scientifique ne vient que d'Allemagne, l'Angleterre ne peut à cause de Dieu, que Bacon, son législateur, respecte, adopter la science pure.

Here, Mallarmé is obviously interested in the mystic or intuitive side of Descartes—the Rosicrucian who discovered his new analytic geometry in a sort of trance; the author of a project of universal grammar (letter to R. P. Mersenne, 20 November 1629), etc.—which he senses to be in his own absurdist lineage; that is the *science pure* that he at first denies to Germany and England, then seems to grant to Germany, possibly because of Hegel (although I think he got little very specific from him). At any rate, his *langage mathématique* and interest in mathematics here is not the sort of mathematics he rejects in *Igitur*.

The reading "mathématiciens et pirates" (in *Documents Mallarmé*, no. 6, 1977, p. 445) makes no sense; nothing in the text confirms it; *expirâtes* is likelier and leads to the contrasting absolute project of Igitur, the lone metaphysical survivor.

Devais finir: this imperfect tense, looking forward, is another example of the looping or spiraling approach that embraces past and present, extreme consciousness and unconsciousness, in a tetrapolar (and polypolar) fusion, *absolu* or *Infini*.

Simplement: this is made very clear just below, in this passage.

Quant: may refer backward to the *parole* that explains Igitur's enterprise to his ancestors (in terms of his relation to them), or it may refer forward to the next section, where he addresses them in similar terms (more probably the latter).

Rien: (a) since Igitur is the last descendant, the ancestral line will disappear entirely; (b) ambiguously, the ancestors' sentimental and undefinitive vision will give way to the new, absolute vision. Vigny, in *l'Esprit pur*, said of his ancestors: "A peine une étincelle a relui dans leur cendre. . . . Tous sont morts en laissant leur nom sans auréole. . . . Seul et dernier anneau de deux chaînes brisées, / Je reste. . . ." Mallarmé goes a step farther than Vigny; even their ideas, or books, are vain from now on.

L'infini enfin: the infinite here is what always eluded the ancestors who, failing to accept it deeply, unlike Igitur, were dominated by it in the form of trivial time-becoming, or *le hasard*. He, on the contrary, rediscovers the old absolute—old "space," without time-becoming, without chance (or so he thinks).

Elle a eu raison: the family was right to deny the infinite (or chance leading to it) and to exist in this way —incompletion was its normal existence, *sa vie*, as usual (cf. the *Fiançailles*, which is this same "horizontal" becoming, flirtation with the All throughout history, on Page 5 of the *Coup de Dés*)—so that the infinite, as the absolute, was left in its original unsullied state (*ait été*), and Igitur could be the one to act unprecedentedly, purely.

Ceci devait: the absolute is the relatively static, or Being, pole of this couple; *l'Infini* (with a capital *I*) is the kinetic, or Becoming, pole. Their dialectical relations produce all the "combinations"—children-phenomena through time—including this last definitive one, the final dice throw gesture of Igitur, crowning all the rest.[5]

5. In his *Notes*, Mallarmé uses somewhat different terms. First he sees *fiction*, or *jeu*—paradox—as the very procedure of thought (p. 851); in subsequent passages he sketches the relation of the various terms of his (linguistic, or rather epistemological) philosophy. We can sum this up as follows in our polypolar scheme, which is basically his.

Nécessaire: this idea of a fated, crowning act is discussed above. The *Idée* is an upper-pole (formal, mental) expression of the total absolute; at times the *Idée* stands for the absolute, though Mallarmé usually offsets this "idealism" with more complex formulations, as we have seen in preceding pages. In other words, he is not a pan-logicist in the Hegelian way, but closer to Kierkegaard and his ontological and paradoxical "scandalous" concerns, which criticize the Hegelian universe, offset its synthesis with "antisynthesis," as we noted in the introduction.

_____

L'Absolu (Être), or Macro-Totality (Infinite)

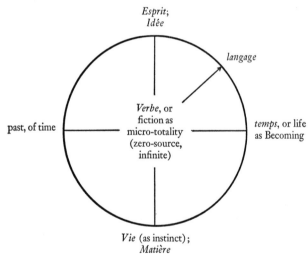

NOTE: *Verbe* is a "principe qui se développe à travers la négation de tout principe, le hasard" (p. 854). Thus, as a source-fiction, *Verbe* vibrates between these negative and positive principles.

All these poles, etc., are fictional. Furthermore, *langage* has two aspects: *parole* and *écriture*; *écriture* is a particular combination of "Idea" and "gesture" (material) that gives more permanency to the combination of Idea and matter in *parole*.

Folie utile: the absurd aspect will have "paid off," recalling the praise of folly that we find in Montaigne, Erasmus, and a whole tradition discussed by Foucault and others. We note that *Hamlet* reflects a madness topos in the Renaissance period.

Un des actes: clear. The act is not alienated from all; it is objective, organic, as Mallarmé and most good poets want to be, the very voice of the Creation, like the sound of the cricket Mallarmé describes in a letter to Lefébure (17 May 1867) or the *impersonnel* passage in his letter to Cazalis of 14 May 1867, cited earlier.

Plus rien: the crowning act involves a fusion of *parole* (mental) and *geste* (physical) in that *souffle*, thus achieving the *tertium quid* that momentarily seems to bring off an objective It or synthesis in the Hegelian sense.[6] But, precisely, Mallarmé will not stop there but, through "antisynthesis," in the pattern of Kierkegaard, open up the play of thought again, ad infinitum, as testified by the incompleteness of his *conte* . . .

The *bougie de l'être par quoi tout a été* means that the candle, as opposed to book (light opposed to dark, etc.), is an expression of the duality that is the essence of life as becoming or existence (*été*, as opposed to the unitary *Absolu*).[7]

6. This phenomenological entity is in a long tradition of overcoming the Cartesian duality, including Hegel, Coleridge, and the modern phenomenologists, also R. Blackmur: language = "psychic gesture."

7. This ambiguous use of *été* is like that of the existential dialectic of Sartre in *L'Être et le Néant*: it is only through *néantisation* (parallel to Igitur's acceptance of death and chance) that Being loses its impure existence in the sense of *das Man*, *doxa*. *Été* is used in this way in the "de trop" passage of *La Nausée* (at the end of which the existential *être* shifts to the ontologically pure usage "I wanted to *be*").

Preuve: a sort of proud Q.E.D. Igitur will have demonstrated something definitive. Or so he thought then. The next line, *Creuser tout cela*, indicates, however, that even here he is not so sure . . .

(D)

I

LE MINUIT

Certainement subsiste une présence de Minuit. L'heure n'a pas disparu par un miroir, ne s'est pas enfouie en tentures, évoquant un ameublement par sa vacante sonorité. Je me rappelle que son or allait feindre en l'absence un joyau nul de rêverie, riche et inutile survivance, sinon que sur la complexité marine et stellaire d'une orfèvrerie se lisait le hasard infini des conjonctions.

Certainement: the absolute act is approached, anticipated, or rehearsed, in most of the remaining text, beginning here.

Igitur believes he has achieved a stasis of resolve, symbolized by the "Midnight when the dice are to be thrown" of the preceding section (C). Here he has already focused on that Midnight, and the essence of that zero-point experience is still with him, he feels, thus perhaps reinforcing in time—which seems arrested through that *persistence* of the zero experience—the sense of stasis.

L'heure: the essence of time—*L'heure*—the absolute point of it, has not disappeared, for example through a mirror: ordinarily, contemplating that magic piece of furniture would mark a diversion in which time would have gotten away from Igitur *through* the mirror, as in *Hérodiade*, where the mysterious depths seem to plunge into a past of memory. Another corollary possibility of its flight would be through burying itself in the curtains; the elusiveness of time, sounding in a meaningless ordinary way—*vacante sonorité*—would serve only to bring out the externality of the "piece of furniture," which is the clock and perhaps by extension the other pieces of furniture, mirror and curtains.

Je me rappelle: contrariwise, as Igitur wanted it, fixed, time would be just a zero point, a *joyau nul* of sound—here the *vacante sonorité* seems to paradoxically turn into the desired neutrality of zero, *nul* (*T.P.*, p. 215). This image from the preceding sentence is picked up in the echo effect so typical of Mallarmé's poetic universe and rife in this text despite its "coolness"—of *sonore* (*sonorité*) and *son or*, ambiguously implying a golden sound and the gleam of decor on a clock. The *inanité sonore* of *Ses purs ongles* is parallel to the *vacante sonorité* here in the sense that both refer to something coldly, neutrally superior that stands out (homeopathically) against the dark of meaninglessness, although the former refers to a sort of trinket, a hollow shell with the probable familiar roaring sea sound in its emptiness, and not a clock sound. The sonnet plays extensively with the *or* element, as does the present text: it is the nucleus of the mere gleam, the vestigial presence subsisting in a world of chance, like the *blanc cheveu* of *À la nue accablante tu*, the mere wisp of foam, which the clock gleam becomes here, too.

The latter image, implying emanating externality quite explicitly—the absence becomes presence before you know it—leads swiftly to the image of a strung-out *orfèvrerie* like a constellation or a reflected (symmetrical) image of constellatory foam, i.e., multiplicity, the "hasard infini des conjonctions," all that Igitur is trying to avoid now.

That sea-sky opposition is often, for Mallarmé, the duality of existence as it emerges from a paradoxical unity —an epistemological phenomenon described in Eliphas Lévi, *Dogme et rituel de la haute magie*: "Le binaire est l'unité se multipliant d'elle-même pour créer" (p. 64). This pattern is important in the *Coup de Dés*, where the cosmogony begins with the preceding and concludes with the reverse, cf. "La mer, dont mieux vaudrait se taire que l'inscrire dans une parenthèse si, avec, n'y entre le firmament" (p. 403); see below: "Les constellations et la mer, demeurées, en l'extériorité, de réciproques néants."

se lisait: the Bonniot text had "lisaient," an obvious error of Mallarmé.

(E)

Révélateur du minuit, il n'a jamais alors indiqué pareille conjoncture, car voici l'unique heure qu'il ait créée; et que de l'Infini se séparent et les constellations et la mer, demeurées, en l'extériorité, de réciproques néants, pour en laisser l'essence, à l'heure unie, faire le présent absolu des choses.

In the past just contemplated (D), revealing a true midnight (the lowercase *m* has no significance discernible), the clock (or sound of it) never indicated that *conjoncture* whence arose the emanation or flight of the external reality, the Becoming marked by the two poles of sky and sea.

Since they are understood as safely outside, Igitur's absolute remains uncontaminated.

(F)

> Et du Minuit demeure la présence en la vision d'une chambre du temps où le mystérieux ameublement arrête un vague frémissement de pensée, lumineuse brisure du retour de ses ondes et de leur élargissement premier, cependant que s'immobilise (dans une mouvante limite), la place antérieure de la chute de l'heure en un calme narcotique de *moi* pur longtemps rêvé; mais dont le temps est résolu en des tentures sur lesquelles s'est arrêté, les complétant de sa splendeur, le frémissement amorti, dans de l'oubli, comme une chevelure languissante, autour du visage éclairé de mystère, aux yeux nuls pareils au miroir, de l'hôte, dénué de toute signification que de présence.

Et du Minuit: here Igitur is no longer so sure: the absolute moment becomes a hesitant one in which his thought and memory "shiver."

It is still a would-be static moment in which things are fixed—"become themselves," as in the "privileged moments" of poetry or art[8]—arresting his thought and perception, but not quite.

8. Thus the ordinary flower of Mallarmé's "Crise de vers" and Malraux in the Kama episode of *La Condition humaine* gives way to an essential, truer flower of art (or privileged vision), "realer than real." Note that the duality of the "referent" here

lumineuse brisure . . . premier: a polarity of knowing,
seen now in the form of expansion and contraction (parallel to Baudelaire's *vaporisation-centralisation*): Igitur's
mind or perception spreads out into the world and returns, canceling itself, leaving a fringe of neutral light
gleams out there, like indifferent constellations left over
after the rise and fall of mankind, as in the *Coup de Dés*.
But the gleams still vibrate, like not-so-cold stars (the
Coup de Dés says this too—[constellation] *froide . . .
pas tant*—on its last page); the absolute is not yet, as life
goes on . . .

Cf. "arrêt des cercles vibratoires de notre pensée," a
"limite suprême" (p. 852).

The *immobilisation* of time is corollary: the previous
phenomenon of time (*chute de l'heure*) is canceled by
a present one, remembering the first, and the *moi* is the
pure calm narcotic stasis in-between, again not so pure,
hence in a *mouvante limite*.

The *moi*[9] is also the micro point of space (as well as
time), as opposed to the peripheral macro of the gleams

---

reflects the Saussurian duplicity of the sign. See my *Modes of
Art*, p. 36.

9. In this vibrant *moi* (*mouvante limite*), the first and last
paradox of epistemology is present, as it will be explicitly later
—"il y a et il n'y a pas de hasard," etc.—that is to say, the
vibrancy that Igitur detects at the periphery, he is already finding at the core. Although he thinks in later passages that he has
dealt with this problem, in the end it will "get him" in a salutary
way. Then he will see that the vibrancy of paradox is the very
stuff of epistemology, the *Jeu suprême*—"la fiction . . . le procédé
même de l'esprit" (p. 851). Small wonder, then, that he finds it
amidst the "calme narcotique [of the] *moi* pur longtemps rêvé."

In relation to the *moi*, cf. Emerson, "the hero is he who is
immovably centered" (quoted by Baudelaire in *Oeuvres complètes*, Gallimard, 1954, p. 865); as well as Baudelaire's "vaporisa-
tion du moi" (ibid., p. 1206).

"out there." The two dimensions of time and space are already being—vibrantly—related here.

Note that the paradox of circular time here (in memory, canceling movement) is the familiar one of Zeno—the paradox of continuity-discontinuity—or, later, of Valéry (*Le Cimetière marin*).

Mais dont le temps: at this point Igitur seems to approach fixity again; time seems to be stopped in the heavy wall-hangings—the echo *temps-tenture* helps the sense of static objectification, time being *in* the hangings; the *frémissement* seems to be *amorti* there, the gleams of light "completing" the static presence of time in the hangings, adding their still presence and appearing, in their constellatory string, to be like a wavy line of hair[10] around Igitur's face in the mirror (reminding us somewhat of the constellation in the mirror of *Ses purs ongles*). This staring into a mirror is the existential ordeal alluded to earlier, where ordinary reality is undermined; even time seems to disappear, and one sees a horror of depersonalized, frozen (in space and time) essence in one's face, an absurd, unreal "stranger" (as in the mirror experience later described by Sartre in his article on Camus' *L'Étranger* and in a similar episode in *La Nausée*). All that is left is a "visage . . . dénué de toute signification que de présence." The *yeux nuls* are ambiguously both "alike" *in* the mirror and *to* the mirror, for emptiness.

10. The imagined hair of the hero-heir may well owe something to Roderick Usher in Poe's tale, which Mallarmé praised highly (p. 232). Usher is the last of his line, an ultrarefined scion like des Esseintes, who both crowns and carries to extinction his lineage. His refinement, "out of this world," has an objective correlative in his delicate hair, ultimate surreal branching of the family "tree."

(G)

C'est le rêve pur d'un Minuit, en soi disparu, et dont la Clarté reconnue, qui seule
demeure au sein de son accomplissement
plongé dans l'ombre, résume sa stérilité sur
la pâleur d'un livre ouvert que présente la
table; page et décor ordinaires de la Nuit,
sinon que subsiste encore le silence d'une antique parole proférée par lui, en lequel, revenu, ce Minuit évoque son ombre finie et
nulle par ces mots: J'étais l'heure qui doit me
rendre pur.

Depuis longtemps morte, une antique idée
se mire telle à la clarté de la chimère en laquelle a agonisé son rêve, et se reconnaît à
l'immémorial geste vacant avec lequel elle
s'invite, pour terminer l'antagonisme de ce
songe polaire, à se rendre, avec et la clarté
chimérique et le texte refermé, au Chaos de
l'ombre avorté et de la parole qui absolut
Minuit.

Inutile, de l'ameublement accompli qui se
tassera en ténèbres comme les tentures, déjà
alourdies en une forme permanente de toujours, tandis que, lueur virtuelle, produite
par sa propre apparition en le miroitement
de l'obscurité, scintille le feu pur du diamant
de l'horloge, seule survivance et joyau de
la Nuit éternelle, l'heure se formule en cet
écho, au seuil de panneaux ouverts par son
acte de la Nuit: « Adieu, nuit, que je fus, ton
propre sépulcre, mais qui, l'ombre survivante, se métamorphosera en Éternité. »

C'est le: the Midnight is essential, turned into itself (*soi*);[11] ambiguously, it is Igitur's own self as well—there is no clear division of subject and object here. That *soi* is like the instinctual *ombre* into which Igitur will plunge the blown-out candle-light in the supreme moment, hence the *Clarté* is a mere vestige marking the pure moment. As that vestige, signifying nothing, it is "sterile," recalling the *indifférence* and *neutralité* of earlier passages.

The *stérile clarté* is summed up by the pale open book on a table, the *grimoire* with its silent prediction of this moment. In this silence—authentic, pure—returned in the current moment, Midnight expresses its absolute essence, *finie et nulle* (the *ombre* is its vestigial ghost here) through the imagined words: "I was the hour which must make me pure."

Here, the vibrancy of past-present that we saw in the survival of the midnight moment (F) can be seen also as a past-future. The definitive act is yet to come, but in this rehearsal there is an ambiguity—as we noted—of the present and the future. We can simplify this exfoliating paradox as a past-present one.

As we remarked in the outline of the syntactical movement, the attempt to plunge the duality of form and matter into the synthesis fusing light and darkness, etc., is symbolized by the *ombre*, which represents the unconscious, or intuition, where this fusion of opposites might occur.[12] But from this *accomplissement* in shadow there persists the light of the idea of the *accomplissement*, as the restless polarities of life carry on in what

11. Possible overtone of *soie* ("curtains").

12. "Shadow squared," as it were, cf. the earlier *Chaos*, Sartre's *Néant*, Lacan's *manque à être*.

I have called, in previous works, the "kinetic excess," that force whereby life always eventually surpasses our formulations. This is what will sober Mallarmé about his "victory," asymmetric in the sense of denying the polar opposite that always springs up in time through "kinetic excess," such as the devastating "antisynthesis" that offsets synthesis (as in Kierkegaard's "scandal"). Here Igitur is honestly observing the persistence of a *Clarté* that irritates him, though the term *seule* indicates he is belittling the problem it raises; the term *ordinaires* referring to the page of the open book, "decorating" the room and dark Night, is another such defensive maneuver; they seem to have nothing to do with his inner "accomplishment." But the subsistence of the ancient word in the book (*lui*) has to be dealt with, too, in Igitur's usual way of a past-present circle: the present appearance of the word and its original appearance cancel each other, in his mind, just as the Midnight, *revenu* (either *ab origine* or from the static moment of recent memory), is canceled again into absoluteness by the paradox-symmetry of past and present, seen as part of circular time; hence the spiraling formula, in the book and of (about) the book: "I was the hour which must make me pure." The present book speaks from the past and, paradoxically, from the present, hence time flow is overcome.

So we have a series of cognate polarities and of paradoxes dealing with, or fusing, them: past versus present, Midnight past versus Midnight in memory (*rêve pur* is both), prediction versus fulfillment, (understood) ancestors versus Igitur, and so on.

Depuis: the old idea in the—somewhat messianic—prediction has been dead until Igitur resurrects it. The flickering candle-light points to its ambiguity of death-life. The *chimère* is the flickering or ephemeral life-light (to be extinguished); cf. all the disenchanted formulas of art and life itself as *chimère*, "nothing permanent," such as the *glorieux mensonge* of the letter to Cazalis of 14 May 1867, cited earlier. The *chimère* is often the symbol of that deceitful promise for Mallarmé, as it had been for Gautier and others. The extinction will put an end to the dream of the prediction and fulfill it simultaneously. The candle-light is like the hope that kept the prediction—the book—alive and like the death that is its goal, hence the *songe polaire*, vibrant, paradoxical (*antagonisme*).

immémorial: the closing of the book—*le texte refermé*—parallel to the extinction of the candle; these parallel ambivalences are hinted at in the pale flickering light and the pallor of the ignored book and finally will be fulfilled in the *Chaos* when all these opposites are fused.

antagonisme: echoes *agonisé*; both imply the struggle of opposites.

Chaos: a further descent or neutralization, more essential than *ombre*: light and dark are vital polar opposites, whereas what Igitur seeks is something that aborts them, indifference, like the *hasard* and *rien* of the *Coup de Dés* and the earlier-mentioned *indifférence* or *neutralité* in *Igitur* (C). The former polarity of word-deed ("parole et geste") has become "Chaos de l'ombre avorté et de la parole qui absolut Minuit," i.e., a more complex entity: the blown-out candle produces not the mere polar opposite of dark but a Chaos in which that dark is aborted (I suspect *avorté* should have an extra *e*), just as the *parole* that accomplishes Midnight becomes not just a silence—when the book is closed—not a polar opposite, but a *Chaos*.

Inutile: it is the hour that is useless, i.e., canceled, as we have seen, in Chaos. Obviously something goes on, as the text, parallel to the lived experience, goes on; it is the useless hour formulating itself in this "echo": "Adieu nuit, que je fus ton propre sépulcre mais qui, l'ombre survivante, se métamorphosera en Éternité." The hour, in this, is canceling itself anew. Its present vestige (echo) is seen to be merely the tomb of the hour—it is either the tomb-shadow of the *Chaos* into which Igitur has plunged it, or, in a more usual sense, there is a possible meaning that the past phenomenon of the hour is dead in the present one, hence the present says to the past time that I am "your own tomb." But it adds that if the shadow of the death of time survives it will become Eternity, a restatement of the familiar (and vulnerable) dialectic of Igitur: life / accepted death / Life.

The voice of the hour emerges from the furniture, which is *accompli*, i.e., already fixed in the provisional stasis of Igitur's rehearsal, but which will be further neutralized—"se tassera en ténèbres comme les tentures, déjà alourdies en une forme permanente de toujours." The hangings already seem to have become absolute, before the other furniture, probably because they look inert, dark in the dark, especially as when windows are closed in winter or at night. Mallarmé often speaks of their heaviness, influenced by the death-of-hope mid-night atmosphere of Poe's *Raven*, as in the sketched *Sonnet à Wyse* (*T.P.*, p. 221):

> Moi qui vis parmi les tentures
> Pour ne pas voir le Néant seul

> Aimeraient ce devin linceul.
> Mes yeux las de ces sépultures, [*sic*]
>
> Mais tandis que les rideaux vagues
> Cachent des ténèbres les vagues
>
> Mortes hélas. . . .

These *tentures* hide the *Néant* but are close to it in nocturnal tone and suggest shrouds and tombs. No doubt the echo *temps-tenture* and the heavy nasal sound have some bearing too. A tapestry had "plis inutiles" in the *Ouverture ancienne d'Hérodiade*; the "uncertain curtains" of *The Raven*, the *vagues-vagues* of the *Sonnet à Wyse*, and the "plis inutiles" are connected in this one atmosphere of heavy, useless, and hopeless mystery and fate. The rhythm of wall hangings or curtain folds (or tapestry, etc.) is the fundamental "squirm" we find throughout Mallarmé, in his many "folds," each a useless, writhing, agonizing attempt to wriggle out of fate —this is the shape of the *chimère* and of the *ptyx* as I treat them in my commentary on *Toast funèbre* and *Ses purs ongles* (*T.P.*, pp. 96–110, 138–46). Derrida has followed suit with his well-known article on the *pli* in *La Dissémination*.

tandis que: meanwhile, the diamond of the clock survives in the dark and/or the memory of the (rehearsed) "eternal Night" moment, but it too is canceled by its being merely a virtual light, flickering like the candle, produced out of—as an appearance of—the very dark itself as a *miroitement de l'obscurité*, hence extremely vibrant with paradox and unsureness.

The "act" that opens the "panels" of the tomb (of the hour, etc.) is the psychic-suicidal one Igitur is trying out here.

(H)

II

IL QUITTE LA CHAMBRE
ET SE PERD DANS LES ESCALIERS
(*au lieu de descendre à cheval sur la rampe*)

L'ombre disparue en l'obscurité, la Nuit resta avec une douteuse perception de pendule qui va s'atteindre et expirer en lui; mais à ce qui luit et va, expirant en soi, s'éteindre, elle se voit qui le porte encore; donc, c'est d'elle que, nul doute, était le battement ouï, dont le bruit total et dénué à jamais tomba en son passé.

D'un côté si l'équivoque cessa, une motion de l'autre, dure, marquée plus pressante par un double heurt, qui n'atteint plus ou pas encore sa notion, et dont un frôlement actuel, tel qu'il doit avoir lieu, remplit confusément l'équivoque, ou sa cessation: comme si la chute totale qui avait été le choc unique des portes du tombeau, n'en étouffait pas l'hôte sans retour; et dans l'incertitude issue probablement de la tournure affirmative, prolongée par la réminiscence du vide sépulcral du heurt en laquelle se confond la clarté, se présente une vision de la chute interrompue de panneaux, comme si c'était soi-même, qui, doué du mouvement suspendu, le retournât sur soi en la spirale vertigineuse conséquente; et elle devait être indéfiniment fuyante, si une oppression progressive, poids graduel de ce dont on ne se rendait pas compte, malgré que ce fût expliqué en somme, n'en eût impliqué l'évasion certaine en un intervalle, la cessation; où, lorsqu'expira le heurt, et qu'elles se confondirent, rien en effet ne fut plus ouï: que le battement d'ailes absurdes de quelque hôte effrayé de la nuit heurté dans son lourd somme par la clarté et prolongeant sa fuite indéfinie.

The title is clear from our previous remarks; *se perd* indicates a descent into the unconscious dark realm. The "(*au lieu de descendre à cheval sur la rampe*)" suggests a playful touch to this *folie*, in line with a certain infantile quality in Hamlet, reminiscences of his childhood in the scene with Yorick, etc. Igitur "read his lessons" to his ancestors earlier in this innocent spirit.

The puerile tone is expanded in *T. IV*, AC: *Malgré la Défense de sa Mère, allant jouer sur les Tombeaux* and "Ne descend-il pas à cheval sur la rampe toute l'obscurité—tout ce qu'il ignore des siens, corridors oubliés depuis l'enfance." In Mallarmé's translation of Poe's *La Dormeuse* we read: "Quelque haut caveau—quelque caveau qui souvent a fermé les ailes noires de ses oscillants panneaux [cf. the oscillating panels of *Igitur*] . . . quelque sépulcre écarté, solitaire, contre le portail duquel elle a lancé, dans sa jeunesse, mainte pierre oisive . . . frissonnante de penser, pauvre enfant de péché! que c'étaient les morts qui gémissaient à l'intérieur."

In the margin of *T. IV*, AC there is: "Interdiction de sa mère de descendre ainsi—sa mère qui lui a dit ce qu'il avait à accomplir," etc. And in the text proper of *T. IV*, AC: "Autre gaminerie" and "Je ne peux pas faire ceci sérieusement: mais le mal que je souffre est affreux, de vivre." The childish folly of the act does not prevent its seriousness. Life is absurd *and* suicidal . . .

The stairs represent a linear process between two

97

stases—the chamber and the tomb at the bottom—which is a familiar epistemological pattern in Mallarmé, and which I have discussed at length in my *Oeuvre de Mallarmé* (*O.*, p. 288). Its linearity—stairwell or tunnel shape—which will be called "corridor du temps" (II, N) is in the pattern of process or Becoming, and that in itself is a threat to the perfect symmetry of Being (the absolute) he is seeking; the imagery often refers to this phenomenon, which is the main subject of section II. At times it is a flight of a bird, at times an asymmetric "progress" of Igitur himself, and these have to be dealt with through elaborate epistemological strategies that make up much of the text.

The enemy movement of the night-time as bird-flight goes back to *The Raven* or such standard metaphors as Tennyson's "the black bat night has flown" (*Maude*). In the *Noces d'Hérodiade* (*N.*, p. 203) the same fundamental metaphor is evoked in "l'aile échevelée . . . de la nuit." An almost exact parallel to the theme of a sought arrestation of time versus its escaping wing-beat will be deployed by Pierre Reverdy in *Ronde nocturne* (from *Les Épaves du ciel*): "L'heure qui s'échappait ne battait plus que d'une aile."

L'ombre: the shadow is Igitur, plunged into the staircase dark, also the *Chaos de l'ombre* he deliberately became in the last section, the place of fusion of opposites, the (rehearsed) stasis he is seeking. It can also be a reference to the fact that Igitur is now dead, in a sense, a mere shadow. In both senses—it or he—the shadow is plunged further down the stairs leading to the tomb, disappearing thus into *obscurité*; but again the idea of a Night (absolute, *Minuit*) asymmetrically persists and moves in a Becoming through a duality-rhythm (as opposed to the unity of Being). Becoming is felt concretely as pendulum beat (it will turn out to be Igitur's own heart, still going in this "ghost"), which seems to be reaching a realization or localization in him (*lui*; Igitur, the *Il* of the title above) and also an imminent expiration —that is his vestigial all-too-human fear of its stopping, as we soon learn.

mais à ce qui luit: this is the idea (cf. the *Clarté* previously) of the Night that Igitur believes he can fuse back into unity, as with all the other escaping poles that threaten his absolute symmetry. Hence it will "dying in itself, be extinguished," fused back into unity. Yet, *elle* (the Night)—the impersonal entity that alone survives (he believes)—still carries it, the pendulum. Hence, he concludes, it is from the Night itself, the unity, that this duality-*battement* proceeds and was heard, and accordingly he feels that it is no threat to his unity. The noise of the duality accordingly falls back into the unity of time as well, back into the past; as an entity belonging to the unity of the absolute it is *total* and *dénué à jamais*, neutral as was the face of Igitur in the last section.

Note the echoing of *lui-luit, s'atteindre-s'éteindre; elle* has overtones of *aile*, soon to emerge. In all this echoing, the text is rounding on itself poetically as it does epistemologically, as well, seeking a perfect symmetry.

In this last paragraph, according to the pattern I traced in my *Synoptic Syntax*, the series or chain of systoles and disastoles of unity-duality-unity-duality, etc. (at the epistemological level—concretized as various polarities: candle and dark, etc., and now as pendulum, and soon as heartbeat and wing-beat, which are made into unities that open again, etc., etc.); this chain in the following paragraph becomes a spiral (*la spirale ver-*

tigineuse) as it moves toward a tetrapolar (and poly-polar) symmetry. This is what the next paragraph is very specifically about: the *Conte* here in particular is a play-by-play description of the movement of mind itself, of the sort Valéry will make famous in his *Monsieur Teste* and *Agathe*.

D'un côté: Igitur fuses the pendulum-duality (*équi-voque*) in a central unity, but right in the heart of it, at right angles[13]—as we shall soon see—a new duality is being born as the old one dies. This is the *irony* of paradox, creating a new polarity out of the very movement that collapses an old one. For the moment, Igitur makes the distinction merely of "on the one hand, on the other," but the distinction will soon become perpendicular. The new motion, persisting, is also equivocal, since it is a clear and marked double knock, but one that is not fully realized, no longer or not yet; he isn't sure, so that the duality is here between two poles of past and future, and we already have a sketchy tetrapolarity of equiv-ocation, ambiguity, or paradox.

The *frôlement actuel*, a new ambiguous beat, *remplit confusément l'équivoque*, i.e., arises amidst the old po-larity-beat, as we said, in a new dimension of paradox, hence at right angles, to put it schematically. This new phenomenon ambiguously (*confusément*) either fills up and unifies and hence causes to cease the old paradox, or it doesn't; hence, a new doubt and beat arises. This is as if the unified closing of the tomb doors (panels),

13. This right-angle movement of compensation between di-mensions is part of the pattern of distortion of space-time in relativity theory (black-hole theory).

Note also that the movement of body cells, isolated, across a laboratory slide is markedly rectangular, according to a recent scientific study.

which we first saw at the end of the last section, was a duality made unity that opens, in an epistemological doubt, into duality again and so vibrates in paradox (referring back also to the *double heurt* as opposed to the *choc unique*). Thus a duality-unity vibrancy (doors) is crossed by a duality-unity of two moments of attitude toward them: the enclosed, dead, and hence unified "*hôte*" (Igitur) is also not enclosed. He is separated from the dead or death, so he is both in the tomb and out. This is paradox squared, or "tetrapolarity." Hence "la chute totale qui avait été le choc unique des portes du tombeau, n'en étouffait pas l'hôte sans retour."

He then sees that doubt—*incertitude*—is probably caused by the asymmetry of an affirmation, which is "prolonged" by another asymmetry, the memory (*réminiscence*) of the unifying event of the burial of the pendulum noise (overlapping with the *choc* of the tomb's closing) in the previous paragraph,[14] with which memory is confused, *la clarté* playing here exactly the same asymmetric role as it did in the previous section, i.e., it is again and again an idea or perception that violates perfect symmetry, the absolute Igitur is seeking. In the midst of the doubt—the *incertitude*—arises (again at right angles) the paradoxical dimension of tomb panels both open and closed (*chute interrompue*); this interruption Igitur compares to a pivoting of the self, a taking back: as it were, "first I thought they were open, then I see they weren't." This is what I have called "antisynthesis," a fourth term added to the Hegelian triad, which radically cancels a synthesis and is felt to reverse time ("take it all back").

This antisynthetic movement added to the movement

14. Note *heurt*, echoing *heure*, as in the notes published by Bonniot. There it was called a *bruit*, here a *heurt*.

of duality-become-unity (synthesis) sets up a tetrapolar tension. If simultaneous, it is a static cross, but if it moves in time along a time line the play (game) or tension between the four poles naturally becomes spiral, like a dog chasing its tail. However, in this case one dimensional loop is crossed by another dimensional loop, so the spiral is more complex, like the paths of electrons around a nucleus, and is vertiginous in its spinnings of the deep movement of mind caught in a sophisticated form of infinite regress. Hence: "Elle devait être indéfiniment fuyante."

But the regress, as always happens, is stopped by a life impulse, which, in this case, is linked with Igitur's ongoing (and dual, in Becoming) heartbeat, frightened precisely by the endless regress. That impulse first appears as *une oppression progressive*, *poids*, a weight off-setting the light-flight of spinning mind; it is the weight of his "heavy" heart. The weight is "de ce dont on ne se rendait pas compte, malgré que ce fut expliqué en somme," i.e., precisely as an impulse it is not realizable and offsets the too neat symmetry that was spinning infinitely and intolerably.[15]

In that impulse, at first gradually felt, the evasion of the spiral regress occurs as a cessation of it at a sudden turn, an *intervalle*. Now, when the *heurt*—of the tomb closing—is silenced (the spiral arose from that *heurt* and its problematic asymmetry), and now that the oppression and its evasion or cessation are "confused" in one moment of silence,[16] nothing more is heard but the ab-

15. Cf. the similar movement resolving what René Girard calls the endless spiral spin of "mimetic desire." The Oedipal impulse toward an earthly object (woman) is comparable to the heartbeat here.

16. Note the echo *elles . . . ailes*. Also *motion . . . notion*.

surd wing-beat of a bird, "some denizen of the night struck in his heavy sleep by the light and prolonging his flight indefinitely." That impulsive creature, associated with Igitur's frightened heartbeat (with reminiscences of *The Raven*, *Eureka*, and *The Tell-Tale Heart*), is "absurd" because there is no good reason for the fright in Igitur's stoically determined view and resolve. The *clarté* that disturbs the bird is, no doubt, as before, the idea (and possibly candle-light) Igitur brings down with him into the stairs, the persistence of his asymmetric all-too-human mind, which he will dream of eliminating later in a sort of self-decapitation. The flight here is not the regress, but the "evasive" flight of life, like that of the ancestors.

The bird rises organically from the night as in Poe: "the raven wings of midnight" (*Ligeia*) or the raven of the familiar poem. Later, Mallarmé will speak of "l'aile échevelée de la nuit," in the *Noces d'Hérodiade*; cf. Tennyson's "the black bat night" (*Maude*).

Most generally, in Mallarmé, the bird symbolizes, as it does for a long poetic tradition, an impulse to the beyond, aspiration, and hence a hint of the divine. But the dark deathly overtones in the nocturnal aspect of the bird indicate a bitter rejection—as in his early poems on the dead sister or friend—of any easy hope in that direction: "nevermore." The all-too-human "kinetic" and doubting aspect of the bird in *Igitur* reflects that mutation.

Finally, the Poe-inspired detective mood of tracking down an enemy principle through analysis and deduction is especially evident in this section. This is the chess player Poe of the *Murders in the Rue Morgue*, *Marie Roget*, and *The Purloined Letter*, also, in a more *self*-analytic, psychological way, of *The Imp of the Per-*

verse. Mallarmé's *Démon de l'analogie* owed something, indubitably, to the latter, and he is certainly working the vein of subtle obsession here.

(I)

Car, pour le halètement qui avait frôlé cet endroit, ce n'était pas quelque doute dernier de soi, qui remuait ses ailes par hasard en passant, mais le frottement familier et continu d'un âge supérieur, dont maint et maint génie fut soigneux de recueillir toute sa poussière séculaire en son sépulcre pour se mirer en un soi propre, et que nul soupçon n'en remontât le fil arachnéen—pour que l'ombre dernière se mirât en son propre soi, et se reconnût en la foule de ses apparitions comprises à l'étoile nacrée de leur nébuleuse science tenue d'une main, et à l'étincelle d'or du fermoir héraldique de leur volume, dans l'autre; du volume de leurs nuits; telles, à présent, se voyant pour qu'elle se voie, elle, pure, l'Ombre, ayant sa dernière forme qu'elle foule, derrière elle, couchée et étendue, et puis, devant elle, en un puits, l'étendue de couches d'ombre, rendue à la nuit pure, de toutes ses nuits pareilles apparues, des couches à jamais séparées d'elles et que sans doute elles ne connurent pas—qui n'est, je le sais, que le prolongement absurde du bruit de la fermeture de la porte sépulcrale dont l'entrée de ce puits rappelle la porte.

Car, pour: the duality is now seen as a "panting"—rhythm of breath instead of heart—but that changes little; Igitur now associates the flight, and duality, with the duplicity of doubt about his own victory (the absolute, unity) but immediately denies that doubt, comparing its beating flight again to a bird's wings. They now metamorphose, according to his defensive belief, into the strokes of a feather duster wielded by ancestral geniuses of a superior era eager to clean the walls of the stairs—or the "corridor" of tradition leading to him—of all the dust of time and gather it into the "ashes" at the bottom where he will, in the last section, lie down in the dust of the dead. Cf. "la tentative d'une superiorité s'inaugure par étendre, sur des distinctions vulgaires, en les effaçant, aile égale" (p. 413); cf. "le Temps ... frotte [une image] avec son aile" (Baudelaire, *Le Portrait*). The walls are thus polished so Igitur can reflect himself purely in them[17]—the walls will form a tetrapolar symmetrical chamber in which past and present and other pairs reflect each other infinitely as in a set (or two sets, etc.) of opposing mirrors.

se mirer: ambiguously, the ancestors wanted to mirror themselves in a reflecting surface but, further, in their heir, Igitur. *Propre* is likewise ambiguous: their own self (themselves or Igitur as their son-self) and also "clean," the pure self seen in the dust-free walls. Here, the *tabula rasa* of Descartes merges with the "wipe away all fond trivial records" of Hamlet.

nul soupçon: the final apparition will be uncluttered by any cobwebs (or dust), which might, like a line of communication, emanate it linearly in impure becoming, like gossip, Platonic *doxa* or "opinion," etc.

In a letter to Verlaine (*L'Amitié de Verlaine et Mal-*

17. Cf. "[préserver] sa native illumination [en] époussetant quotidiennement l'effort hasardeux extérieur, recueilli plutôt sous le nom d'expérience" (*Mallarmé lycéen*, p. 42).

larmé, Gallimard, 1939, pp. 20–21) we find: "Mon esprit dans sa gaine amassée de toiles d'araignées et de poussière." Here Mallarmé is thinking both of his tired mind and of the crummy room he is moving into, in Besançon; in *Igitur*, this becomes the crud of sentimental centuries that a few superior minds tried to brush off, as we noted. The webs can also refer to networks of too-logical thought, constructs, the old clutter of mind Mallarmé attacks in the *mathématiciens* (C).

Note that dust is visible time (as in a sand hourglass), which Mallarmé wants to overcome. In the *Eventail* (for Mme Mallarmé), his wife performs this role, making for a pure household mirror, maybe his limpid art.

le fil: in the Bonniot text it is *fils*, an obvious error.

pour que l'ombre dernière: here, clearly, the mirroring in the pure walls is of the "last shadow." Igitur is already psychically a ghost, too, joining a procession of ancestral ones, hence the *foule de ses apparitions* refers to this single line of shadows, each one with the polar pair of light and dark, now seen as a "nacreous star of their nebulous knowledge," held in one hand—that is probably a description of the candle—and the book, with its gleaming golden clasp, in the other. It is called the *volume de leurs nuits*, partly because of its mystery and mainly, I think, to bring out the darkness of that pole, as did the black characters in an earlier passage (A). Thus the candle and the book form a light-dark *breadth*-polarity while the ancestral shadows— "telles à présent se voyant pour qu'elle se voie, elle, pure, l'Ombre"—form a *length*-polarity of past-present (or past-future). The *Ombre* is Igitur; the ancestral shadows see themselves in the mirror of the clean walls so that Igitur can see himself in them.

ayant sa dernière forme: the last of the ancestral shad-
dows is behind him, lying prone, *couchée et étendue*
(that last shadow can be an earlier version of Igitur himself, not just ancestrally but in his previous life or even
just a moment ago in the epistemological-dramatic procession of forms). In a ruthless Nietzschean way, Igitur
just steps on or over it. Before him—so that he, the
Shadow, is a nodal point of a polypolarity—in a pit or
"well"[18] of shadow stands a series of shadows symmetrical with the ancestral line, but their reach (*étendue*)
is *rendue à la nuit pure*, i.e., purified by Igitur's act. The
shadows in this line are saved for purity after the act;
these shadows have, as it were, their "glorious body" in
a sort of secular assumption. They are separated from
the old shadows by that difference, and Igitur adds that
"they [the ancestors] didn't know them, no doubt," i.e.,
that they never suspected the possibility of this act.

All the last development began with the dash following *arachnéen* and ended with the dash after *pas*. The
next phrase refers back to the *fil arachnéen*: Igitur feels
that the thread of becoming is a wobbly "absurd" doubt
prolonged by the flitting equivocation about whether
the tomb doors are opened or closed; the thread went
back and the tomb doors lead forward to a future development—*entrée de ce puits*—equally dubious. They
thus form a pair of Becomings that, again, seem to reassure him by their symmetry.

(J)

Cette fois, plus nul doute; la certitude se
mire en l'évidence: en vain, réminiscence
d'un mensonge, dont elle était la conséquence, la vision d'un lieu apparaissait-elle

18. Note the echo *puis . . . puits*.

encore, telle que devait être, par exemple,
l'intervalle attendu, ayant, en effet, pour parois latérales l'opposition double des panneaux, et pour vis-à-vis, devant et derrière,
l'ouverture de doute nul répercutée par le
prolongement du bruit des panneaux, où
s'enfuit le plumage, et dédoublée par l'equi-
voque exploré, la symétrie parfaite des dé-
ductions prévues démentait sa réalité; il n'y
avait pas à s'y tromper c'était la conscience
de soi (à laquelle l'absurde même devait ser-
vir de lieu)—sa réussite.

Cette: he quells; then, *en vain*, he goes over the scene
again, this vision of a place being the "réminiscence d'un
mensonge dont elle était la conséquence." The *glorieux
mensonge* of the cited letter to Cazalis (14 May 1867)
and the "artifice que la *réalité*" of *Un Spectacle inter-
rompu* give the tone of this double self-reflecting fiction, a "vain" memory of a "lying" event, all of which
is in the spirit of Igitur's self-denying act. But here the
double fiction serves the purpose of his "success." It is
"in vain" that his doubt resurrects the scene with its vibrant dimensions of doubt; the symmetry survives these
tests by the very fact that the doubt is itself a fiction
(unlike a parallel moment in Descartes' *cogito*), hence
no sentimental intrusion into this self-sacrificial world
has occurred.

In the vision, Igitur sees the polypolar symmetry,
again self-canceling and very clearly put: the *intervalle
attendu* is that subtle in-between moment when paradoxical dimensions exfoliate one from within the other. The
lateral paradox-dimension is the "pour parois latérales
l'opposition double des panneaux"; the longitudinal par-

adox-dimension is "devant et derrière, l'ouverture de doute nul répercutée par le prolongement du bruit des panneaux," i.e., the (vibrant) doubt in the past echoed (and balanced) by the (vibrant) open-shut doors to the tomb. The bird-flight fled along that line of doubt (in either direction) as we have seen; but now it seems to be accounted for.

dédoublée: this *exploré* and *dédoublée* is the vision above going over again the problems of symmetry: the symmetry reinforced denies the reality of *équivoque*. It is a success. The "absurdity" of the enterprise—life-death—made it possible, gave it a site (*lieu*). (But the absurdity that entered each of Igitur's polarities, as the text does not yet say, will ultimately undermine this assurance).

(K)

Elle se présente également dans l'une et dans l'autre face des parois luisantes et sé-culaires ne gardant d'elle que d'une main la clarté opaline de sa science et de l'autre son volume, le volume de ses nuits, maintenant fermé: du passé et de l'avenir que parvenue au pinacle de moi, l'ombre pure domine par-faitement et finis, hors d'eux. Tandis que devant et derrière se prolonge le mensonge exploré de l'infini, ténèbres de toutes mes ap-paritions réunies, à présent que le temps a cessé et ne les divise plus, retombées en un lourd somme, massif (lors du bruit d'abord entendu), dans le vide duquel j'entends les pulsations de mon propre cœur.

Je n'aime pas ce bruit: cette perfection de

> ma certitude me gêne: tout est trop clair, la
> clarté montre le désir d'une évasion; tout est
> trop luisant, j'aimerais rentrer en mon Om-
> bre incréée et antérieure, et dépouiller par
> la pensée le travestissement que m'a imposé
> la nécessité, d'habiter le cœur de cette race
> (que j'entends battre ici) seul reste d'am-
> biguïté.

Here the symmetrical *conscience de soi—Elle* of the
first line—is again presented, in very clear terms; the opposing ancient walls keep of *elle* (the *conscience*) only
the gleams of candle and book, which are (together
with the side walls themselves) the lateral polarity. The
book is now closed in the suicidal final act (rehearsed).
The past-future dimension is presented, and the nodal
point of the tetrapolarity is the *moi*, the pinnacle. *Du
passé et de l'avenir* means probably that the book and
candle are *of* the past and future, stand for their successive moments.

l'ombre pure: it dominates the cross; it is the pure
shadow of shadows. *Finis* probably refers to the past
and future, now finished off, dominated, fixed. *Hors
d'eux* is the absolute nodal zero, "out of time" (etc.), as
in Proust; note the *x* (as in *O.*, pp. 112–14 or *T.P.*, pp.
276–78).

Tandis que: the Becoming, infinite lie, of shadows
has been explored—lying because of the subjacent total
fiction, lying also because the Becoming was sentimental, ancestral tradition, and lying because it only falsely
threatened Igitur's symmetry. But now that series—the
plurality itself is part of the "life-lie" (as Ibsen would
say, *Lebenslügen*)—is all summed up safely in the *ap-*

paritions réunies, as the rest of the paragraph clearly states and confirms without problem of interpretation: *lourd somme* refers to the massive sleep (*somme*; H) of unity (*Chaos* also, previously; G) from which the frightened bird of doubt and evasion awoke startled; hence also the reference to the *bruit*, the doubt that awoke it. In the reestablished certainty—its *vide* being its purity—the pulsing of the heart, clearly stated, begins anew, at first with uncertain impact.

Je n'aime pas: the heartbeat is once more a doubt, and Igitur doesn't like it. Again he sees the doubt as a function of his very certitude; its symmetry has become a one-sided victory, hence asymmetric. As before, a *clarté* stands out as the manifestation of this, and he desires to plunge that light into shadow, *Ombre incréé*: cf. the *Chaos*, neutral and before time (*antérieure*, ambiguously "primordial" and also "previous," in his mind, to the *clarté*). So he wants to use mind against mind (*clarté*), strip it off for the sake of pure unity and with it the heartbeat that goes with its dubiety, its on-going impurity set up by the asymmetry, the mere Becoming he associates with his lineage, his ancestors, *cette race*. The vestigial "ambiguity" he wants to overcome is like the *Fiançailles* of the *Coup de Dés*, the mild flirtation that ordinary mankind carries on with the absolute throughout their on-going, unfinal lives (*O.*, pp. 215–22).

A precedent of an ambiguous heartbeat finally located in the self is in Poe's *Eureka*:

> a novel Universe swelling into existence, and then subsiding into Nothingness, at every throb of the Heart Divine? And now—this Heart Divine—what is it? *It is our own.*

(L)

A vrai dire, dans cette inquiétante et belle
symétrie de la construction de mon rêve, laquelle des deux ouvertures prendre, puisqu'il
n'y a plus de futur représenté par l'une
d'elles? Ne sont-elles pas toutes deux, à jamais équivalentes, ma réflexion? Dois-je encore craindre le hasard, cet antique ennemi
qui me divisa en ténèbres et en temps créés,
pacifiés là tous deux en un même somme?
et n'est-il pas par la fin du temps, qui amena
celle des ténèbres, lui-même annulé?

(*chuchotement*)

En effet, la première venue ressemble à la
spirale précédente: même bruit scandé, —et
même frôlement: mais comme tout a abouti,
rien ne peut plus m'effrayer: mon effroi qui
avait pris les devants sous la forme d'un oiseau est bien loin: n'a-t-il pas été remplacé
par l'apparition de ce que j'avais été? et que
j'aime à réfléchir maintenant, afin de dé-
gager mon rêve de ce costume.

The doubt arises again in the following form: If the
symmetry itself is problematic, how can he get out of
it, precisely because it is so symmetrical? There are no
more directions (as in outer space, or at zero point).
The two *ouvertures* are probably the past and future
or the two ends of the tunnel of the stairs: one leads
back to the chamber, the other forward through the
tomb doors. But he sees they are equivalent now, *ma
réflexion*[19] (ambiguous sense: a reflection of his own

19. The *x* in *réflexion* seems active; see under *x* in the letter
tables of *L'Oeuvre de Mallarmé* or *Toward the Poems of Mal-*

inner symmetry; mutual reflection of the mirror-walls, or poles of thought); note, again, the X of symmetry.

Dois-je encore: the *hasard* Igitur thought he had vanquished by "swallowing" it is resurgent, the old enemy that created the trivial dualities (and multiplicities) of Becoming as opposed to unitary Being, including the (Cartesian, etc.) duality that made the crude distinction between discontinuity and continuity, "ténèbres et temps créés" (now pacified in a same "sleep"). "Isn't it itself canceled by the end" of those two poles, "time" and "shadows" (representing continuity and discontinuity, or whole and parts, etc.)—the demise of time having brought on that of its fragments? The *chuchotement* is like the earlier *sifflements* (A), a stirring of the ancestral ghostly public and hence of his sentimental fear. But now, *En effet*, he quiets that fear with a reasoning: the evasive looping of the spiral of infinite regress he now feels to be merely repetitive of the one he has already dealt with effectively. He feels safe too about the heartbeat *bruit scandé* and feather stroke *frôlement* that marked his fear and impulse to escape the regress by abandoning the whole project; he reassures himself that *tout a abouti*, nothing can scare him any more; and he claims that the fear which arose in the form of the bird is now far off, replaced by an apparition which had preceded that of the fear episode, the *apparition de ce que j'avais été*. That refers back to the *Ombre dernière* of fragment I a few pages back, which recognized itself in the *foule des apparitions*, i.e., summed them up successfully and thus overcame, precisely, the bird-heart fear.

---

larmé. (Cf. in particular the *x*'s of *Ses purs ongles*; in Mallarmé's letter concerning that poem the word *réflexion* is central [*T.P.*, p. 138]).

Now he suspects this, too, "reflects" upon it lest it be an asymmetric pole also, a mere form as opposed to unified essence: hence he is suspicious of that apparition and its possible mere outer guise or *costume*, cf. *travestissement* (K). We are reminded of Hamlet's suspicion of mere "trappings and suits" (of woe).

(M)

Ce scandement n'était-il pas le bruit du progrès de mon personnage qui maintenant le continue dans la spirale, et ce frôlement, le frôlement incertain de sa dualité? Enfin ce n'est pas le ventre velu d'un hôte inférieur de moi, dont la lueur a heurté le doute, et qui s'est sauvé avec un volètement, mais le buste de velours d'une race supérieure que la lumière froisse, et qui respire dans un air étouffant, d'un personnage dont la pensée n'a pas conscience de lui-même, de ma dernière figure, séparée de son personnage par une fraise arachnéenne et qui ne se connaît pas: aussi, maintenant que sa dualité est à jamais séparée, et que je n'ouïs même plus à travers lui le bruit de son progrès, je vais m'oublier à travers lui, et me dissoudre en moi.

He continues to reassure himself: the beating (now called a *scandement*, a rhythmic beat) was that of the evasive self, who was frightened of the infinite regress that developed from the self-canceling polarities involved in the perfect symmetry of the reflecting chamber and, in that evasion linked to an asymmetric progress down through the stairwell-corridor, reverts to a duality of Becoming as opposed to the unity of the absolute. This explication marks a metamorphosis of imagery again, in a lengthening chain of such substitutions: the polarity, after being identified with heartbeat, wing-beat, and feather strokes, is now just an abstract duality or progress (Becoming).

The image of the bird recurs: its "doubt" (flight-beat) was aroused by the (asymmetric) candle-light (previously *clarté*, now called a *lueur*). But the light, he now thinks, didn't disturb a bird at all—that "inferior guest of myself" (in the sense of inhabiting his breast, identified with his heart or cowardly flight instinct) who flew off with a flutter, but rather the light disturbed, not that creature's "hairy stomach" but the velvet bust of a member of a superior race (superior to the "inferior" bird's species, hence not cowardly, fleeing) who is bothered by the light (because that superior creature, Igitur himself, rejects the light's asymmetrical appearance) and who breathes in a stifling air—the rarefied air of the absolute—a personage whose thought has no consciousness of himself (hence no duality).

The velvet bust—the *costume* Igitur is wearing, no doubt of aristocratic black, Hamletlike (as Mallarmé imagined him, spurred by contemporary actors and Delacroix)—is referred to at the end of the preceding passage. That image of himself, without duality, he calls his *dernière figure* (as we have seen previously) and now defines it as "separated from his person by a spidery ruff." The separation of the "figure" from the "person" implies precisely a depersonalization; it is a figure "qui ne se connaît pas." Hence, its duality having been dealt with definitively ("à jamais séparée," i.e., separated from the unified figure just described) and the noise of its progress no longer being heard (another victory over a duality, the asymmetric progress of Becoming, with its upsetting "noise," which we have seen in previous passages) Igitur can say confidently "I will forget myself" through that figure, sink into the unconscious unity and "me dissoudre en moi."

The ruff and the velvet-clothed upper body are together the *costume* he mentioned at the bottom of the preceding passage. The spidery quality of the ruff is another metamorphosis of imagery in this multiply self-reflecting text: the spider webs in the stairwell, which represented impure accretions on the polished surface of pure mind and which earlier seemed related to gossipaceous strands of Becoming, threads of conventional and empty verbiage, *doxa*, are now related to those threads woven into a texture, a cloth of outer trappings, of a costume.[20] This image series is partly duplicated in *Salut* (*T.P.*, p. 36). A similar development is found in *La Musique et les lettres*: "Nulle torsion vaincue ne fausse ni ne transgresse l'omniprésente Ligne espacée de tout point à tout autre pour instituer l'idée; sinon sous le visage humain, mystérieuse, en tant qu'une Harmonie est pure" (p. 648).

The idea of a Line menacing a Harmony is parallel in the two texts. And the reference to *torsion(s)* is like the looping spiral of regress in the struggle to overcome the Line (like an evil serpent or twisting, deceitful *Chimère*) in both texts, except that in *Igitur* Mallarmé

20. Cf. "Au collet de cette robe [noire] blanchissaient des poils longs et soyeux, semblables au rabat des savants. . . ." (*Mallarmé lycéen*, p. 341). The separation of head and body is at least remotely (or deeply) connected with the saints/martyrs decapitation (and castration) theme in Mallarmé, particularly the St. Jean parts of the *Noces d'Hérodiade* (*T.P.*, p. 87). The threads of the ruff, secreted like the milk of the "sacred spider" (letter to Cazalis, 14 May 1867), join in the *blancheur* network I discuss in Appendix A of *T.P.*, also *T.P.*, p. 216.

thought he had reached a symmetry through will. In the later essay he is more resigned, and the Harmony comes only with the defeat of will. The "sous le visage humain" corresponds to the knocking down of asymmetric idea in *Igitur*; but the later text proceeds even farther in this negative or resigned direction.

(N)

Son heurt redevient chancelant comme avant d'avoir la perception de soi: c'était le scandement de ma mesure dont la réminiscence me revint prolongée par le bruit dans le corridor du temps de la porte de mon sépulcre, et par l'hallucination: et, de même qu'elle a été réellement fermée, de même elle doit s'ouvrir maintenant pour que mon rêve se soit expliqué.

L'heure a sonné pour moi de partir, la pureté de la glace s'établira, sans ce personnage, vision de moi—mais il emportera la lumière! —la nuit! Sur les meubles vacants, le Rêve a agonisé en cette fiole de verre, pureté, qui renferme la substance du Néant.

Il quitte la chambre

The doubt returns: the noise, or shock—of the closing tomb doors echoing along the *corridor du temps* and the stairwell (or corridors leading to or from it, all part of the linear transition toward the end)—which sets up the doubt, the Becoming-flight, now comes back with its duplicity, *chancelant* (as opposed to firm unity) as it was before he got the pure *perception de soi* at the end of the last section. It was (in fragment I) the beating (*scandement*) of *ma mesure*—his own duality as metonymic, measured progress, or heartbeat—"whose reminiscence came back to me prolonged by the noise in the corridor of time of the door of my tomb, and by hallucination." Again he is reassuring himself as to the cause of that impure Becoming; but once more he thinks he has accounted for that impurity. This reoccurrence of it is only a reminiscence (as in fragment J) of something he had already accounted for (in I). To that previous account he now adds hallucination as an explanation of why his anxiety is baseless.

corridors: in the childish-poetic imagination, this is a spooky realm outside the safe, warm room; ghosts wander there. It is the place of transition literally and poetically, to and from another world, who knows? So, in *Toast funèbre*, Mallarmé chides those who believe sentimentally in an afterlife, saying he will not offer a toast to the "spectre du corridor." Likewise, in *Tout Orgueil fume-t-il du soir*, a revenant would, "naturally," return along the *corridor* or *couloir*, but won't . . .

et de même que: the tomb door was really closed—the resolve to die was firm—and the victory was sure, but now Igitur provisionally opens it again, reopens the static symmetry for another critical investigation, "pour que mon rêve se soit expliqué," i.e., for the sake of a comment on the remaining part of the adventure, to follow. The narrative goes on . . .

In the next paragraph, the reference to "Il quitte la chambre" (in the margin) and the mirror and other furniture all indicate that this fragment belongs to the earlier episode, in the Midnight room; I do not know how it got to be in this spot.

L'heure a sonné: the Midnight ringing of fragment I, with the resolve to leave this world, psychically or truly —it is not always certain, as we shall soon see.

The purity of the mirror will be established when Igitur is gone, will no longer contain his image (*vision de moi*). Yet he thinks he will carry off with him the candle-light, symbol also of his life, his consciousness, without which there will be only night in the mirror. On the empty furniture—emptied of human presence already in a sense, through his cold resolve—the Dream has agonized in this glass phial, purity, which contains the substance of the *Néant*. This phial holds (as is confirmed later) poison, the "substance of Nothing," as it did in the early poem, *Les Fleurs*. The phial itself might be like the *ptyx* of *Ses purs ongles* (where a Master also has departed) on a piece of the furniture (in *Ses purs ongles*, on the *crédence*), but the sentence says rather that the "Dream has agonized" on the furniture, i.e., has fallen in a deathlike fixity described in earlier fragments. The Dream agonized *in* the phial, i.e., drowned in its poison.

In *Surgi de la croupe et du bond*, we have a phiallike vase in whose rounded base (*croupe*) there is a deep dose of *Néant*. This shape of linear *col* and round base is profoundly meaningful in Mallarmé: the base is holistic, ambivalent, "religious" in aspects (Being); the linear *col* is more narrowly human (Becoming). The shape corresponds to the "phallic"[21] erectness of the human (the spinal column, etc.) versus the rounded ("total") emotional source or base (in belly or lower). Cf. a mercury column in a thermometer, with the reservoir or source in the little round glass base; there, real zero and totality occur. The *i* and *o* of *fiole* support this dialectic of line and circle, "male" and "female," so that the idea of fusion of opposites is embodied subtly in this word,

21. Not principally sexual, of course, though that is its undertone (cf. decapitation versus castration).

as in the anagram *folie*, which clearly echoes it, especially in a later passage (T).

(O)

III

VIE D'IGITUR

Écoutez, ma race, avant de souffler ma bougie—le compte que j'ai à vous rendre de ma vie—Ici: névrose, ennui, (ou Absolu!)

Heures vides, purement négatives.

J'ai toujours vécu mon âme fixée sur l'horloge. Certes, j'ai tout fait pour que le temps qu'elle sonna *restât* présent dans la chambre, et devînt pour moi la pâture et la vie —j'ai épaissi les rideaux, et comme j'étais obligé pour ne pas douter de moi de m'asseoir en face de cette glace, j'ai recueilli précieusement les moindres atomes du temps dans des étoffes sans cesse épaissies. —L'horloge m'a fait souvent grand bien.

(Cela avant que son Idée n'ait été complétée? *En effet, Igitur a été projeté hors du temps par sa race.*)

Écoutez: we have seen all this before: the "lesson" read to the ancestors; the axial equivalence of vertical and horizontal "death" and, likewise, Life. Boredom and neurosis, on a flat plane, are ordeals leading eventually to the victory of the absolute, as much as does the deep form of death, the plunge into the tomb. In the margin, the notation; "*Heures vides, purement négatives*," refers again to the "horizontal" ordeal.

J'ai toujours vécu: this narrative account is addressed to the ancestors:[22] Igitur describes his homeopathic struggle against time, his staying with time until it yields a victory; hence the "âme fixée sur l'horloge." He explains that he did this precisely to arrest time ("pour que le temps qu'elle sonna restât présent dans la chambre, et devînt pour moi la pâture et la vie." The *pâture* is Time as positive substance, "nourishment," and "life," the result of his victory over it. He goes over once more the devices for achieving this: thickening the curtains (no longer the *tentures* of the earlier passage), staying very much in (inward). Here, he sits before the mirror for a more human purpose, also recounted in the correspondence: when, after his horrible experience of the *Néant*, Mallarmé was afraid he was disappearing, he told his friend Cazalis (May 1867) that he had to look at his reflection to reassure himself he was still alive. In this version, as is soon confirmed, the *moindres atomes du temps* that Igitur gathers preciously are the motelike appearances one sees in the air or in a mirror when one has stared overlong, particularly in the dusk.

The *étoffes sans cesse épaissies* refer directly back to the progressive thickening of the curtains: this is obviously a symbol for sinking deeper and deeper into his claustral mood. And he repeats the point about the good he gets from this clock nourishment.

In the parentheses, Igitur questions whether this episode precedes the completion of his Idea—in the next fragment we see that this means the conception of his project (one suspects, in Mallarmé's case, based on the

22. Rimbaud looks back to his Gallic ancestors in much the same spirit of seeking his own meaning through time, though he doesn't address them there (*Saison en enfer*). In *Comédie de la soif* he does speak to them, in their tombs or graves.

evidence of the correspondence, that there is no clear beginning). In italics, finally, "*Igitur has been projected out of time by his race*"; meaning, the whole ancestral line led to this final son and to his deed, which takes him out of the line, the irreversible Becoming, time itself.

(P)

Voici en somme Igitur, depuis que son Idée a été complétée: —Le passé compris de sa race qui pèse sur lui en la sensation de fini, l'heure de la pendule précipitant cet ennui en temps lourd, étouffant, et son attente de l'accomplissement du futur, forment du temps pur, ou de l'ennui, rendu instable par la maladie d'idéalité: cet ennui, ne pouvant être, redevient ses éléments, tantôt, tous les meubles fermés, et pleins de leur secret; et Igitur comme menacé par le supplice d'être éternel qu'il pressent vaguement, se cherchant dans la glace devenue ennui et se voyant vague et près de disparaître comme s'il allait s'évanouir en le temps, puis s'évoquant; puis lorsque de tout cet ennui, temps, il s'est refait, voyant la glace horriblement nulle, s'y voyant entouré d'une raréfaction, absence d'atmosphère, et les meubles tordre leurs chimères dans le vide, et les rideaux frissonner invisiblement, inquiets; alors, il ouvre les meubles, pour qu'ils versent leur mystère, l'inconnu, leur mémoire, leur silence, facultés et impressions humaines, —et quand il croit être redevenu lui, il fixe de son âme l'horloge, dont l'heure disparaît par la glace,

ou va s'enfouir dans les rideaux, en trop plein,
ne le laissant même pas à l'ennui qu'il implore
et rêve. Impuissant de l'ennui.

Voici: the completion of Igitur's Idea is the new view
he has of his race and himself since he conceived his
project, his resolve.

Le passé: in terms of the project, his racial past has
taken on a meaning which weighs on him: he carries
the burden of its absolute meaning, which is *fini*, fixed.
Similarly, the (horizontal) clock time, through his ordeal of boredom, became "heavy, stifling." Those sac-
rifices together with his waiting for the accomplishment of (in) the future make a "pure time," or boredom
(neutral, indifferent as the absolute), "made unstable
by the sickness of ideality," i.e., the old all-too-human
urges of the race and self to believe in something ideal,
asymmetrically sentimental, such as afterlife or other
hope.[23]

That instability infects the Being (*être*) of the ennui,
and it disintegrates into multiple phenomena, like the
"atoms of time" Igitur spoke of earlier, which he tried
to fuse. These phenomena are what he will, a bit later,
release from the closed furniture (drawers, etc.), which
are now "full of their secret." Igitur feels threatened, as
in the fright-flights of the last section, by the "torture
of being eternal," which he feels ahead, vaguely. As in
the previously mentioned episode of the correspondence, he seeks reassurance in the very mirror that he
had frozen into boredom in his ordeal and where he had

23. As Camus will repeat in his *Mythe de Sisyphe*, which
Sartre rightly sees in his preface to the *Poésies* (Gallimard) as
being in Mallarmé's lineage.

become likewise vague and ready to disappear, as if he were about to vanish, or faint, into empty time; he "calls himself up" (*s'évoquant*) out of that void.

puis: having gotten himself together again from "all that boredom, time," he sees the mirror horribly empty, and finds himself surrounded (as in section I) by a "rare-faction, absence of atmosphere"—all part of the experi-ence we know from too-fixed staring—and watches the "furniture twist its chimaeras in the void." Those twist-ing lines of the ornate décor of the period, often animal in inspiration, were associated by Mallarmé with the squirm of agony arising from absurd fate (cf. *Ses purs ongles*, *Tout orgueil*, etc.). Igitur observes "the curtains shivering invisibly, unquiet"—shades of the "uncertain / curtains" of *The Raven* (that vestigial uncertainty—like the *mal d'idéalité* above—will disappear in the next sec-tion).

alors il ouvre: he lets out those diversions of varied sorts in order to exorcize, provisionally, the absolute: "leur mémoire, leur silence, facultés et impressions hu-maines." This is like the return to a familiar poetry that Mallarmé sought after his bout with the *Néant*, as we see in his letters: "J'ai commis le péché de voir le Rêve dans sa nudité idéale, tandis que je devais amonceler entre lui et moi un mystère de musique et d'oubli. . . ." (20 April 1868, to Coppée).

et quand: now that Igitur is reassured, he dares to return to his quest of the absolute, fixing his gaze on the clock whose time goes through the mirror, magically arrested in the way we have seen, burying itself in the curtains, being *trop plein*, i.e., as if the time had piled up in its arrestation and spilled over, into the mirror and the curtains (which accords with the familiar experience of too high a psychic charge, spilling out). Accordingly, the time does not stay still and allow Igitur to nourish himself on its boredom (from which he still seeks the absolute), which boredom he "implores and dreams of" in the sense of desiring to break through it to victory. The momentary failure—caused by the instability of time—makes him call himself an "impuissant de l'ennui." One feels that, in addition to this specific kind of impotence, Mallarmé is thinking of the more general impotence that accompanied his stretches of boredom until inspiration, his art, consented miraculously to pierce through it into expression.

(Q)

Il se sépare du temps indéfini et il est! Et ce temps ne va pas comme jadis s'arrêter en un frémissement gris sur les ébènes massifs dont les chimères fermaient les lèvres avec une accablante sensation de fini, et, ne trouvant plus à se mêler aux tentures saturées et alourdies, remplir une glace d'ennui où, suffoquant et étouffé, je suppliais de rester une vague figure qui disparaissait complètement dans la glace confondue; jusqu'à ce qu'enfin, mes mains ôtées un moment de mes yeux où je les avais mises pour ne pas la voir disparaître, dans une épouvantable sensation d'éternité, en laquelle semblait expirer la chambre, elle m'apparût comme l'horreur de cette éternité. Et quand je rouvrais les yeux au fond du miroir, je voyais le personnage d'horreur, le fantôme de l'horreur absorber peu à peu ce qui restait de sentiment et de douleur dans la glace, nourrir son horreur des

suprêmes frissons des chimères et de l'in-
stabilité des tentures, et se former en raré-
fiant la glace jusqu'à une pureté inouïe, —
jusqu'à ce qu'il se détachât, permanent, de la
glace absolument pure, comme pris dans son
froid, —jusqu'à ce qu'enfin les meubles, leurs
monstres ayant succombé avec leurs anneaux
convulsifs, fussent morts dans une attitude
isolée et sévère, projetant leurs lignes dures
dans l'absence d'atmosphère, les monstres fi-
gés dans leur effort dernier, et que les rideaux
cessant d'être inquiets tombassent, avec une
attitude qu'ils devaient conserver à jamais.

Il se sépare: a breakthrough: he is. This is a beauti-
fully definitive, crystallized passage, *Igitur* at its best
and very close to its maker as we know him elsewhere,
even warm, in its coolly understated way. *Sépare* recalls
the *séparer* of *Hérodiade, Scène*, and other definitive de-
tachments: the *opéré vivant* of the Rimbaud essay, the
rupture franche of St. Jean.

Et ce temps: in this passage, time will not be arrested
simply in the furniture or the curtains, but more cen-
trally and effectively in Igitur himself, in his image in
the mirror. The "time will not as formerly stop in a
grey shivering on the massive ebony whose chimeras
closed their lips with an overwhelming sensation of
finiteness." This was obviously too external; the shivering (like the rustling of the curtains, as we have seen)
is a sign of incompletion. The chimeras closing their lips
is an obscure reference to specific animal forms on the
furniture; it suggests that he could expect nothing from
those external mute forms. The same happens with the

heavy curtains, "saturated" with time: there is no breakthrough in that direction either or, for the moment, in
the mirror filled with boredom where "stifled and suf-
focating, I begged to remain a vague figure who was
disappearing entirely confused in the mirror." His aim
is precisely ambiguous: he is afraid of disappearing and
yet knows that only through that sacrifice will he win,
and so his ambivalent begging accords with a double
wish. And he gets his bolder wish.

jusqu'à ce qu'enfin: finally having put his hands over
his eyes in order not to see the vague figure disappear
in a horrible sensation of eternity, in which the room
seemed to expire, the figure appeared to Igitur—"me"—
as the horror of that eternity. That is the final moment
of the ordeal. There is an effective echo of *horreur-
miroir*.

Et quand: "And when I opened my eyes in the depths
of the mirror, I saw the horror-person, the fantom of
horror, absorb bit by bit whatever remained of sentiment and pain in the mirror"—i.e., Igitur took into himself sacrificially all the remaining all-too-human sentiment (or sentimentality and mere human emotion, such
as pain), and it seemed to enter into him, nourish his
ever more rarefied image as he stared courageously. The
vestigially uncertain or unstable curtains and the hes-
itantly shivering furniture also were absorbed into that
final fixity, more and more stubbornly rarefied "to an
unheard-of purity," until the image detached itself, permanent, from the mirror, absolutely pure, as if caught
in its cold. One thinks of the superior, resigned swan of
the "divine" sonnet. The overtone series of *glace* ("mirror"-"ice"-"glass") is at work here, as in many of Mal-

larmé's central poems (see *T.P.*, pp. 128–29 and my "Mallarmé's Windows," in *Yale French Studies*, no. 54, 1977).

Even the items of furniture finally seem to have mercifully ended the shivering death agony of their *chimères*, with their convulsive twisting serpent-loop forms, and they become fixed in their last effort in the empty atmosphere of the absolute; the curtains stop rustling uncertainly and also fall into a final "attitude," "forever."

(R)

IV

LE COUP DE DÉS
(*AU TOMBEAU*)

Bref dans un acte où le hasard est en jeu, c'est toujours le hasard qui accomplit sa propre Idée en s'affirmant ou se niant. Devant son existence la négation et l'affirmation viennent échouer. Il contient l'Absurde—l'implique, mais à l'état latent en l'empêche d'exister: ce qui permet à l'Infini d'être.

Le Cornet est la Corne de licorne—d'unicorne.

Mais l'Acte s'accomplit.

Alors son moi se manifeste par ceci qu'il reprend la Folie: admet l'acte, et, volontairement, reprend l'Idée, en tant qu'Idée: et l'Acte (quelle que soit la puissance qui l'ait guidé) ayant nié le hasard, il en conclut que l'Idée a été nécessaire.

—Alors il conçoit qu'il y a, certes, folie à l'admettre absolument: mais en même temps

il peut dire que, par le fait de cette folie, le
hasard étant nié, cette folie était nécessaire.
A quoi? (Nul ne le sait, il est isolé de l'humanité.)

Tout ce qu'il en est, c'est que sa race a
été pure: qu'elle a enlevé à l'Absolu sa pureté, pour l'être, et n'en laisser qu'une Ideé
elle-même aboutissant à la Nécessité: et que
quant à l'Acte, il est parfaitement absurde
sauf que mouvement (personnel) rendu à
l'Infini: mais que l'Infini est enfin *fixé*.

Here Igitur has emerged from the linear stairway into
a static place, the *tombeau*, site of the final and decisive Act.

The paragraph in italics is an account of the epistemological breakthrough that is Mallarmé's crucial
contribution to twentieth-century thought, as I have
noted in the Introduction, referring to my full study
of the influence in "The Mallarmé Century." I offered
an outline of the new epistemology in those early pages,
showing the crossing or multiplying process of tetrapolarity, involving paradox "squared" (paradox of paradox, the absurdity of the absurd, and so on), and of
polypolarity, which goes farther in the same vertiginous
direction.

The present statement may well imply that at this late
juncture, Igitur-Mallarmé has grave doubts about his
ultimate victory; its incidental, afterthought nature appears in its positioning and style.

Essentially, it tells of the same infinite regress that
set up the evasive flight (of bird or of human heart . . .)
in various passages, but here it is put in clearer, stripped,

epistemological terms. We can summarize the statement as follows.

The phrase "devant son existence [du hasard] la néga- tion et l'affirmation viennent échouer" is a first dimen- sion of dilemma, antinomy, or paradox; *hasard* is the equivalent of the dilemma itself, the Absurd, as it clearly says. One rediscovers this dilemma in the following phrase, "il [le hasard] contient l'Absurde—l'implique, mais à l'état latent et l'empêche d'exister," i.e., the first relationship (negation-affirmation) is summed up as an absurdity, and this summing-up is both affirmed and de- nied, for "contient l'Absurde" is an unequivocal affirma- tion but "l'empêche d'exister" contradicts it firmly. The word *latent* (exists and doesn't exist) is the summing-up of the latter dilemma, as the absurd (in *hasard*) is the summing-up of the first dilemma. The whole formula can thus be epitomized as being "the absurdity of the absurd," an initial dilemma crossed by another level of itself.[24]

The little word *jeu* is the zero-infinite nodal point at the core of this tetrapolar pattern—a most Mallarméan word, whose significance for his later definitive poetic universe takes a major leap here.

The meaning of "ce qui permet à l'Infini d'être" rein- forces one half of the second dilemma, the "l'empêche d'exister," i.e., it is the nonabsurd aspect of chance that creates concrete Infinity, the endless procession of phe- nomena in ordinary Becoming.

The statement seems to give a primacy to *hasard*, which will be pursued in the later work, particularly

24. Chance is arational, but the absurd is more deeply so in the sense that it is aggravated, dialectically, by the meaningful propositions that it "scandalously" negates, as in total contra- diction of two propositions, both true.

"Un coup de dés jamais n'abolira le hasard." That celebrated line, at least superficially, says much the same thing: it is always chance that has the last word. Here we detect some doubt about Igitur's whole enterprise. Below, he says "Mais l'acte s'accomplit," the act that he had just put in grave doubt. But the debate goes on, as we shall see . . .

Le Cornet est la Corne de licorne—d'unicorne: this idea is loosely attached to the idea of the dice throw, from a dice horn, which Mallarmé chooses to be the magic one taken from a unicorn. That seems fitting since the two-one fusion occurs in that horn, i.e., the wavering implied in the expression "the horns of a dilemma," or the sentimental duality of life-becoming, seems resolved in that phallic, spiritually potent entity.[25] I discuss this at length in the Introduction.

The traditional association of the unicorn with virginity is important because Mallarmé's mirrored hero and heroine (Hérodiade) are both virginal, youthful, alone. The element *corne* is connected with the idea of a dice throw, as we said, and also with its cosmic equivalent, as in the *Coup de Dés*, the cosmogonic poem, where there is an initial outburst of stars from this horn (*cornet à dés*), a cosmic womb in that case, so that we have an inner-outer male-female paradox at the origin of All. The outburst is an *issu stellaire* (Page 9, cf. *O.*, pp. 238, 409–10). This can relate to the constellations referred to throughout *Igitur*.

Another facet is the element *or*, which goes well with its use in *Igitur*—for a gilt frame, as well as stars, as in

25. Possible sources for the unicorn, etc., are discussed in André Vial, *Mallarmé*, Corti, 1976, pp. 28–35. See also Richard, *l'Univers imaginaire de Stéphane Mallarmé*, p. 216.

Quand l'ombre (many *or*'s, see also *Ses purs ongles*). To repeat, all this is treated in extenso in earlier pages.

Mais l'Acte: then Igitur accepts (*reprend*) the Absurd, *la Folie*, thus manifesting his courageous *moi* sacrificially, as we saw in the beginning pages of the detailed analysis. "He admits the act" and "voluntarily takes up again the Idea, as Idea"; and "the Act (whatever the power that guided it) having denied chance, he concludes that the Idea was necessary." The Idea was the conception of the project that the act, the dice throw, was to consummate; since the Act was to defeat chance by accepting it—dialectically, homeopathically, sacrificially—it proves that the Idea was necessary. "Whatever power guides it" refers to the tricky *hasard* and indicates that, despite its infinite-regress twisting or looping through polypolarity, Igitur is now confident that he has tamed that elusive chimerical creature, regardless of its "power."

Alors il conçoit: Igitur confesses that it is madness to admit the Idea (and Act) absolutely, since it is based on paradox, absurdity; yet, dialectically, the madness was necessary, since by "swallowing" the absurd the Idea defeats chance (which contains the absurd, as Mallarmé noted above). "[Necessary] to what?" he queries. And answers: "(Nul ne le sait, il est isolé de l'humanité)." His momentary doubt is somewhat absurd, one feels, by virtue of the fact that, as he puts it, no one knows anything in this realm "isolated" from the usual run of men's thoughts, as Igitur himself is isolated.

Tout ce: Igitur has saved his race by his projected Act, made it "pure." His race, through him, has taken away—through the admission of chance, the absurd—

the purity of the absolute, in order, dialectically, to be it, leaving only (behind, as a possible impurity, but which Igitur decides isn't one) "an Idea, itself ending in Necessity . . ." That is, the Idea as an asymmetric pole (formal) might be impure as such, but since it leads to a unifying act, as we have seen earlier, it is not a threat to his perfection.

et que quant à: the Act is perfectly absurd except for the personal movement that launches it, which could be construed as another imperfection (this time material, not formal), but it too is "given back to the Infinite," i.e., by a conversion or sublime "double take"—in the spirit of Nietzsche's "obedience" or Heidegger's *Geworfenheit*—it is seen as a part of everything, not as a separate movement. Note that the "Infinite" in this case is used as synonymous with the absolute or Eternity, as it was used in the early fragment C. That Infinite, or absolute, "is finally fixed." This is a bit like the proud boast of Hegel's universal Idea in which everything is "panlogically" and dialectically understood (at one point Hegel thought it was all coming to a head in his time!). This boast is vulnerable indeed, as we have seen. But there is something to it—a stubborn attempt like this one is at least memorable . . .

(S)

Igitur secoue simplement les dés—mouvement, avant d'aller rejoindre les cendres, atomes de ses ancêtres: le mouvement, qui est en lui est absous. On comprend ce que signifie son ambiguïté.

Il ferme le livre—souffle la bougie, —de son

SCÈNE DE
THÉÂTRE,
ANCIEN IGITUR

*Un coup de dés
qui accomplit
une prédiction,
d'où a dépendu*

133

la vie d'une race. « Ne sifflez pas » aux vents, aux ombres—si je compte, comédien, jouer le tour—les 12— pas de hasard dans aucun sens.

Il profère la prédiction, dont il se moque au fond. Il y a eu folie.

souffle qui contenait le hasard: et, croisant les bras, se couche sur les cendres de ses ancêtres.

Croisant les bras—l'Absolu a disparu, en pureté de sa race (car il le faut bien puisque le bruit cesse).

Race immémoriale, dont le temps qui pesait est tombé, excessif, dans le passé, et qui pleine de hasard n'a vécu, alors, que de son futur. —Ce hasard nié à l'aide d'un anachronisme, un personnage, suprême incarnation de cette race, —qui sent en lui, grâce à l'absurde, l'existence de l'Absolu, a, solitaire, oublié la parole humaine en le grimoire, et la pensée en un luminaire, l'un annonçant cette négation du hasard, l'autre éclairant le rêve où il en est. Le personnage qui, croyant à l'existence du seul Absolu, s'imagine être partout dans un rêve (il agit au point de vue Absolu) trouve l'acte inutile, car il y a et n'y a pas de hasard—il réduit le hasard à *l'Infini*—qui, dit-il, doit exister quelque part.

Scène de Théâtre: this marginal note indicates a possible dramatic project, which, however, obviously didn't get very far and was subsumed into the dramatic aspect of the narrative *Conte*. Mallarmé's dramatic projects generally—the *Faune*, *Hérodiade*—moved toward this monologual intimacy.

Un coup: the prediction in the *grimoire* is briefly alluded to. At the end of this note Igitur pronounces the prediction, ritually, but adds that he doesn't give a fig for it. "Il y a eu folie." That ironic, mocking tone comes out of the *folie* itself: if the project involves swallowing the absurd to beat it, small wonder that the whole project seems finally a *folie* and the prediction itself laughable. As Mallarmé said in the last section, chance and its absurd *folie* always get the last word . . .

Meanwhile, in the marginal note, the " 'ne sifflez pas' aux vents, aux ombres—si je compte, comédien, jouer le tour" indicates more theatricality, with the ancestor-public hissing, as we mentioned in the comment on fragment C. The term *comédien*, along with the *moque* below, indicates also the ironic tone that arises here, reminiscent of Hamlet's, the player who was so conscious of the play.

le tour—les 12: as we noted earlier, the 12 is visually a fusion of 1 and 2 at a Midnight of the mind, end of cycle, etc., on top of the rigidly upright two needles fused into one on the clock face, also a 12 on the dice, which is rare and a winning number.

In the *Coup de Dés* this becomes *l'unique Nombre qui ne peut pas être un autre*, the supreme formula which would dominate fate. In its twelve syllables (as noted in *O*., p. 174, n. 44) there may be a reminiscence of the alexandrine. But, contrary to Mitsou Ronat and his *Change* group (see 'Le Coup de Dés Maintenant," *Europe*, August-September 1980, pp. 159–67), this number does not figure in the title, the pagination, etc., of the *Coup de Dés*; they are obviously forcing things.

No *hasard* in any direction, Igitur claims, from his throw or Act (*tour*; *tour de force*). That was the purpose from the beginning . . .

Now the main passage:

Igitur secoue: the gesture of the final Act involves a movement that Igitur feels is no threat to the perfection (it is "absolved"). One understands the meaning of its ambiguity, i.e., the absurdist ambiguity of accepting chance to defeat it is a dialectic that absolves the movement of the Act. The absurd can take care of any problem in this way—at a steep price, he will again discover (the absurdity of the absurd, etc.). Then he will lie down in the ashes of his ancestors, canceled out, null.

Il ferme le livre: as seen earlier, he closes the book, thus negating all the black characters of sentimental utterance from the past, killing off that tradition with his own psychic (or real?) suicide. The candle is blown out likewise, canceling the brightness side of the polarity. The breath that unifies the word and deed in previous passages is here said to have contained chance (recall the double *ou* of *souffle*, *doute*); it is the dark (outside, wind, fearsome forces) that, simply, obliterates the light. Since, like the *mouvement*, it too needed absolving, the *souffle* was a last link in a chance-becoming. Igitur crosses his arms, lies down in the ashes.

Croisant les bras: that is an act of cancellation (like an x-shape, up crossed by down), indifference, as announced in an early fragment (C). It reflects the tetrapolar symmetry, which Igitur, also earlier (J), called the place of "perfect certitude."

The absolute has disappeared as an external and been absorbed into an internal "purity of his race," as he said in the preceding fragment (S). It must be so since the *bruit*—which previously had set up the flight of evasion —has stopped.

Race immémoriale: the ancestors (Mallarmé used the terms *ancestralement* and *immémorial* on Page 5, the page of Becoming, or history, in the *Coup de Dés*) whose sentimental and vain chronological time was a heavy burden, now fallen into the past, from being thickened or piled up (in Igitur's arrestation) and spilling over (as previously through a mirror or into curtains). The burden is done with, now that Igitur has come. The race, full of imposed chance, lived only for this future, him, their hero.

Ce hasard: the chance was denied by an "anachronism," a time-denying dialectic, abolishing ordinary chronological time of the ancestors; a person (Igitur), supreme incarnation of that race—who feels in himself, thanks to the absurd, the existence of the absolute—has, alone, forgotten the human word in the magic book and the thought in a light, one announcing that negation of chance (this was the prediction of the absurd act canceling chance by its acceptance), the other illuminating the dream as it had evolved (the candle was the Idea, thought, accompanying the action). We are reminded again of Hamlet's "Wipe away all fond trivial records."

Mallarmé uses "anachronism" in a very similar way in his *Notes* (p. 854): Thought arises from Idea by a negation of the latter's becoming in time. (See also "Louis Bertrand . . . un anachronisme a causé son oubli" [*Corr.* I, p. 199], meaning he was out of [before] his time.)

Le personnage: Believing only in the Absolute, he imagines he is living fictively, in a dream as in "Artifice que la *réalité*" (p. 276). He acts "in Absolute terms." But now he finds the act—as opposed to the dream—useless, for "there is and isn't chance." Here again, in the heart of his triumph, is the old "absurdity of the absurd" turning his absurd act into a meaningless one. *Hasard* is, practically speaking, the absurd (chance contained or implied it, Igitur said a bit earlier); and it is crossed by a clear dilemma in which the first absurd (chance) both exists and doesn't, i.e., another dimension of the absurd arises and makes the act itself useless. And yet this does not seem to discourage him; it just seems to make the act pointless—as in Camus' remarks in *Le Mythe de Sisyphe* on there being no reason to commit suicide because of the absurd, since at the moment of death the absurdist dilemma itself disappears, and that was his *raison d'être*.[26] But Igitur's dream, the project, is not abandoned. The act reduces chance to the Infinite, i.e., as a specific gesture, it sets up a concrete equivalent of chance, the endless becoming-procession of phenomena, of which this is one. That Infinite "must exist somewhere," which makes it too concrete for his dream of the Absolute.

(T)

V

IL SE COUCHE AU TOMBEAU

ou les dés—
hasard absorbé

Sur les cendres des astres, celles indivises de la famille, était le pauvre personnage, couché, après avoir bu la goutte de néant qui manque à la mer. (La fiole vide, folie, tout ce qui reste du château?) Le Néant parti, reste le château de la pureté.

This is the aftermath of the Act. Igitur is dead, either literally or psychically. The "ashes of the stars" imply that, as James Joyce put it, "When I go all goes." This is a sort of *dies irae*, "solvet saeclum in favilla"; Mallarmé also referred to this cosmic final day in *Toast*

26. Camus reencounters this pattern in the initial pages of *L'Homme revolté* and abandons his earlier (at least momentary) belief in the absurd (not just suicide but the absurd itself is deeply questioned in those later pages).

funèbre: "L'heure commune et vile de la cendre." The family's ashes—the earlier terms *race* and *ancestors* have become this humbler expression "family," for no apparent reason—are also, more obviously, involved in the tomb setting. Igitur here is said to have drunk the "drop of Nothing which is missing from the sea." That is clearly a reference to suicidal poison; the drop missing from the sea is a part-whole relation, the part that rejoins an individual to the all in death (and thus itself rejoins the total "sea"). (See *O.*, p. 153.)

La fiole vide: the empty phial is itself a microcosmic version of Igitur's *château*, which in turn stood for the whole human habitat or the world. In the *Coup de Dés*, with the disappearance of man, his final Work is left behind, momentarily, like a tombstone monument, then it too vanishes in eternal mist. It is called a *faux manoir*, echoing the *châteaux* and any other container of man, like the shell-like *ptyx* of the sonnet or the *squames* on Page 8 of the *Coup de Dés*, man's pathetic animal attempt to protect himself from fate. This container, or monument, extends from the tiny phial to the human cosmos as dwelling place, all finally shrunk to nought in the final pages of the *Coup de Dés*, leaving ultimately only the distant constellation as a possible germ of rebirth, of survival of meaning. Here this pattern is not fully worked out, merely suggested in the *fiole* (and the anagram *folie*, which implies the madness of any hope of prevailing over absurd fate, as well as Igitur's desperate Act, which he called *folie*). The *fiole-château* link hints at the later development. With the *Néant* gone —drunk up (just as Igitur noted earlier that he and his race absorbed the absolute, parallel to the "swallowing" of chance to defeat it)—there is this *château de la pureté*,

the objective little phial standing for complete indifference, neutrality, like the "cold" and "distant" final stars
of the *Coup de Dés*. In the *Coup de Dés* Mallarmé will
go the next step and have even this *château-fiole* entity,
which still is redolent of humanity, disappear in mist.

The "dice—absorbed chance" (in the margin) is another version of the neutral objectivity left behind. In
that indifference, as we have seen, chance is defeated by
its homeopathic absorption, the suicidal Act. There is
an implication that the dark spots of number on the dice
disappear into pure monumental blocks, confirmed by
fragment AD: "Le temps . . . qui créa se retrouve la
matière, les blocs, les dés—"

III

Touches (*Scolies*) and Commentary

IN THESE REWORKINGS of the main text we will occasionally skip passages that merely duplicate previous ones. But there is a great deal that is new, and some of it throws light on obscure meanings.

(U)

TOUCHES

I

L'heure a sonné—certainement prédite par le livre—ou, la vision importune du personnage qui nuisait à la pureté de la glace chimérique dans laquelle je m'apparaissais, à la faveur de la lumière, va disparaître, ce flambeau emporté par moi: disparaître comme tous les autres personnages partis en temps des tapisseries, qui n'étaient conservées que parce que le hasard était nié par le grimoire, avec lequel je vais également partir. O sort! la pureté ne peut s'établir—voici que l'obscurité la remplacera—et que les lourds rideaux tombant en temps, en feront les ténèbres, —tandis que le livre aux pages fermées toutes les nuits, et la lumière le jour qu'elles sép-

141

arent. Cependant, les meubles garderont leur
vacance, et agonie de rêve chimérique et pur,
une fiole contient la substance du Néant.

Et maintenant il n'y a plus qu'ombre et
silence.

Que le personnage, qui a nui à cette pureté
prenne cette fiole qui le prédisait et se l'amalgame, plus tard: mais qu'il la mette simplement dans son sein, en allant se faire absoudre
du mouvement.

L'heure: in the first five lines, little is added to what
we know: the "person . . . harmed the purity of the
chimerical mirror" in the sense of having to disappear
in order to achieve the absolute;[1] "chimerical" mirror
because it is a mirage of hope and beauty like all the
other deceitful appearances of an absurd fateful world,
cf. the "O miroir" of *Hérodiade*.

The "autres personnages partis en temps des tapisseries" are figures in the wall tapestries now dead as
Igitur wills to be, thus pure (cf. the *Mages* and sibyls
of the *Ouverture ancienne d'Hérodiade*, *T.P.*, p. 60).
The *temps* is a fixed eternal time of the sort he seeks.

The *ou* in line two may well be really an *où*, as Rolf
Stabel notes.

qui n'étaient conservées: the figures in the tapestries
were "conserved," despite having "left," because of the
sentimental denial of chance by the *grimoire*, the an-

---

1. Igitur is *de trop* in the same sense that Sartre's Roquentin
is in *La Nausée*. "Nausea" is a sort of morning sickness preceding
a (creative) rebirth. Igitur's equivalent is mortal *ennui*. This
theme of rebirth is central to Mallarmé (*Le Pitre châtié*, *Hérodiade*, *Une dentelle s'abolit*).

cestral book, with which Igitur will also "leave," i.e., by his closing of it, which will offset the denial of chance.

O sort: he doubts: the purity he seeks will be replaced by darkness, with darker shadows in it of heavy curtains. Becoming will persist in the alternation of pages, which, closed, form nights, and the candle-light, which represents the intervening days (previously the polarity was of black characters and light).

Cependant: nothing new. We see again the *rêve chimérique*, the mirage of hope, through Igitur's Act, of prevailing, finding meaning in an absurd universe. This could mean he doubts his Act itself and, indeed, there is much more of this touch of "antisynthesis" throughout *Igitur* than critics used to believe, as I have noted earlier.

Que le: the *fiole qui le prédisait*: that object was there, in its materials at least, before Igitur, following the cosmogonic Becoming that will be developed in the *Coup de Dés*; as there, it will be left over, like the stars, when he is gone. He puts off the final drinking of the poison. Now, all he does is put it in his bosom (of the velvet doublet, no doubt) and go to have himself "absolved of the movement" in a dialectic we have seen before.

Here, we intercalate a fragment published by the review *Les Lettres*, in their special Mallarmé number of 1948. It duplicates much of the substance of *I: Le Minuit* but in a more lyric vein, unusual and indeed almost unique in the *Conte* as we have it. Igitur apostrophizes the clock:

Longtemps, oh! longtemps, quand tu sonnais en vain, maintenant une atmosphère d'absence, ton son d'or revenait à toi, dans ma rêverie et t'y créait, joyau d'or, et jeté en m'indiquant sur ta complication stellaire et marine, les occurences externes du jeu des mondes; mais je puis dire, faisant allusion aux souvenirs d'une race que tu évoques, que jamais, sur ces surfaces qui marquent les jeux multiples et combinés de la multiplicité de la pensée universelle, jamais, résumé de l'univers que tu es, joyau des choses, tu n'as fait une minute d'une aussi magnifique concordance et je doute que cet instant ait dans le présent son pareil, parmi l'indicible multiplicité des mondes. Ma pensée est donc recréée, mais moi, le suis-je? Oui, je sens que ce temps versé en moi me rend ce moi, et je me vois semblable à l'onde d'un narcotique tranquille dont les cercles vibratoires, venant et s'en allant, font une limite infinie qui n'atteint pas le calme du milieu.

Longtemps: Igitur looks back to previous moments that anticipated the present climactic Midnight. When the clock sounded in vain, in that dehumanized climate he seeks again, "maintaining an absent atmosphere," (accordingly) "your golden sound came back to yourself in my revery"—this is the cyclic pattern of memory, the cancellation of progressive time he wants—"and created you there" (in his revery, out of time, as it were) as a "golden jewel," static, perfect (echoing the jewel of the works).

jeté: modifies *joyau d'or* (as in "minuit jeta son vain nombre" of *Sonnet pour votre chère morte*): "Sounded, indicating to me on your marine and stellar complication the external occurrences of the play of worlds." This has all been explained before: this is the external macrocosmic version of the drama in the room and mind of Igitur.

mais je puis dire: he thinks of the ancestors whom this clock—as an heirloom—"evokes" and reflects that never in all that "play" of time and space, all those (dice throw) "combinations," never did you, the clock—you "résumé of the universe" (microcosm), "jewel of things" (in that same sense of microcosm, condensation of reality)—"you never made a minute of such magnificent concordance [i.e., convergence of reality on one representative moment or act], and I doubt if this instant has any like it amidst the unspeakable multiplicity of worlds." Here, Igitur thinks he is unique in this world and all possible worlds.

Ma pensée: the preceding meditation is the *pensée*, recreated thus in a fullness of presence, but Igitur queries: "Am I [recreated]?" He wants to be reborn whole, obviously, not just as a thought. He answers his own question in the affirmative: the *temps* that poured into him in his ordeal of boredom, "sweating out" time and thus neutralizing it, has ended in a victory of self, permanent and calm. This is compared to the effect of a tranquil narcotic with circular waves of feeling going out and returning into him in an expansion and contraction characteristic of the psyche (as described by Baudelaire in his *Journaux intimes*, unknown to Mallarmé). This diastole-systole is "vibrant" with the instability of becoming, as opposed to the calm center, moving outward to what Mallarmé had previously called *une mouvante limite*, here *limite infinie*, ceaseless waves to a same point, which indicates the endless multiplicity of life "out there" as opposed to the sure node of self; compare "comme en pleure la rive . . . jeu monotone" of *Prose (pour des Esseintes)* (*T.P.*, p. 253) and the meaningless waves at the end of the *Coup de Dés*.

(V)

II

PLUSIEURS ÉBAUCHES
DE LA SORTIE DE LA CHAMBRE

Γ

Les panneaux de la nuit ébénéenne ne se refermèrent pas encore sur l'ombre qui ne perçut plus rien que l'oscillation hésitante et prête à s'arrêter d'un balancier caché qui commence à avoir la perception de lui-même. Mais elle s'aperçut bientôt que c'était en elle, en qui la lueur de sa perception s'enfonçait comme étouffée, —et elle rentrait en elle-même. Le bruit, bientôt, se scanda d'une façon plus définitive. Mais, à mesure qu'il devenait plus certain d'un côté, et plus pressé, son hésitation augmentait d'une sorte de frôlement, qui remplaçait l'intervalle disparu; et, prise de doute, l'ombre se sentait opprimée par une netteté fuyante, comme par la continuation de l'idée apparue des panneaux qui bien que fermés, ouverts encore cependant, auraient, pour arriver à cela, dans une vertigineuse immobilité tourné longuement sur eux-mêmes. Enfin un bruit qui semblait l'échappement de la condensation absurde des précédents s'exhala, mais doué d'une certaine animation reconnue, et l'ombre n'entendit plus rien qu'un régulier battement qui semblait fuir à jamais comme le volètement prolongé de quelqu'hôte de la nuit réveillé de son lourd sommeil: mais ce n'était pas cela, il n'y avait sur les parois luisantes aucune trame, à laquelle pussent s'attacher même les pattes arachnéennes du *soupçon*: tout était luisant et propre; et si quelque plumage avait jamais frotté ces parois, ce ne pouvait être que les plumes de génies d'une espèce intermédiaire soucieuse de réunir toute poussière dans un lieu spécial, afin que ces ombres, des deux côtés multipliées à l'infini apparussent comme de pures ombres portant chacune le volume de leurs destinées, et la pure clarté de leur conscience. Ce qu'il y avait de clair c'est que ce séjour concordait parfaitement avec lui-même: des deux côtés les myriades d'ombres pareilles, et de leurs deux côtés, dans les parois opposées, qui se réfléchissaient, deux trouées d'ombre massive qui devait être nécessairement l'inverse de ces ombres, non leur apparition, mais leur disparition, ombre négative d'eux-mêmes: c'était le lieu de la certitude parfaite.

This passage duplicates fragments H, I, and J of section II and needs little additional comment.

Les panneaux: the panels not being closed refers to the fact that Igitur is not yet in the tomb (*ébénéenne* is a new term, changing nothing essential, though, as we noted, it seems to catch the tone of Elbehnon). The "shadow" (Igitur, in his ancestral line of shadows), *elle*, gradually locates the *balancement* in itself—the *perception s'enfonçait*, sinks into the self in this sense. The *frôlement* is a duality of Becoming filling the two-beat *scandement* (at right angles); as one closes, the other opens. The unity of self (heart) and external beat is the cessation of the hesitation between these two poles; this is the *intervalle disparu*, that ceased hesitation, which is replaced, as we said, by the *frôlement*. All this is familiar from earlier fragments. The polypolar hesitation starts the infinite regress, which leads to the oppressive vertigo of simultaneously open and closed doors, which seem to turn on themselves, in a sort of spiral become whirl. From this regress, his impulsive fear-flight arises, expressed as *l'échappement de la condensation absurde des précédents*, the natural flight from the spiral regress of paradoxical polarities. At first it is identified with a bird-flutter, but that is quickly denied. No "suspicion" (cf. the "doubt" that earlier upset his symmetry) can dirty his clean walls of pure thought; no webs are there for suspicion to cling to like a spider of doubt and Becoming (thread-spinning). Again we see the ancestral geniuses with their feather dusters keeping the walls clean for their heir—they are *intermédiaires*, this time, leading to him as ancillaries, not yet full geniuses like him—and they are collecting the dust in a special place (the tomb?) so that the tetrapolar chamber of the stairwell can form a perfect symmetry: the line of shadows each with its polar pair of candle and book, extended by the polarity of the laterally reflecting mirrors (walls), provide one (spatial) dimension; at right angles to that are the shadows of the shadows, the longitudinal dimension (time), with the "holes" at back and fore of the tunnel as poles. The perfect certitude of tetrapolarity, in sum. All this we have seen before, except for the few noted nuances of expression. Note: *eux-mêmes* refers, in the last line, to *côtés*, probably.

(W)

L'ombre n'entendit dans ce lieu d'autre bruit qu'un battement régulier qu'elle re-

connut être celui de son propre cœur: elle
le reconnut, et, gênée de la certitude parfaite
de soi, elle tenta d'y échapper, et de rentrer
en elle, en son opacité: mais par laquelle des
deux trouées passer? dans les deux s'enfon-
çaient des divisions correspondantes à l'infini
des apparitions, bien que différentes: elle jeta
encore une fois les yeux sur la salle qui, elle,
lui paraissait identique à soi, sauf que de la
clarté la lueur se mirait dans la surface polie
inférieure, dépourvue de poussière, tandis
que dans l'autre apparue plus vaguement il y
avait une évasion de lumière. L'ombre se dé-
cida pour celle-là et fut satisfaite. Car le bruit
qu'elle entendait était de nouveau distinct et
le même exactement que précédemment, indiquant la même progression.

As in the earlier text (J), the *certitude parfaite* seems
too pat. It is an affirmation, therefore one-sided, asymmetric; so a new flight begins, seeking a new unity
(*opacité*). Again, the symmetry leaves doubt as to which
way to go: the file of shadows goes off infinitely in
both directions, "same" (*correspondantes*) and "different." Now Mallarmé forgetfully speaks of a *salle* instead
of a stairwell-tunnel. Yet there are the two *trouées* that
are the past and future poles of the path of his progress;
Igitur hesitates between them. But he now distinguishes,
unprecedentedly—in a momentary move toward polypolarity (adding a high-low dimension to the previous
tetrapolar lateral symmetry)—between a lower polished
surface and an upper one where the light is vaguer, and
he chooses the latter for his escape. This is, no doubt,
because the darker surface is a place of *opacité* where

he can drown his *certitude (trop) parfaite*. This solution satisfies him momentarily: now he seems to have understood what the beating noise was; it is all part of a pattern that he develops in the next paragraph—it is all the *même progression*.

(X)

Toutes les choses étaient rentrées dans leur ordre premier: il n'y avait plus de doute à avoir: cette halte n'avait-elle pas été l'intervalle disparu et remplacé par le froissement: elle y avait entendu le bruit de son propre cœur, explication du bruit devenu distinct; c'était elle-même qui scandait sa mesure, et qui s'était apparue en ombres innombrables de nuits, entre les ombres des nuits passées et des nuits futures, devenues pareilles et extérieures, évoquées pour montrer qu'elles étaient également finies: cela avec une forme qui était le strict résumé d'elles: et ce froissement quel était-il? non celui de quelqu'oiseau échappé sous le ventre velu duquel avait donné la lumière, mais le buste d'un génie supérieur, vêtu de velours, et dont l'unique frisson était le travail arachnéen d'une dentelle qui retombait sur le velours: le personnage parfait de la nuit telle qu'elle s'était apparue. En effet, maintenant qu'il avait la notion de lui-même, le bruit de mesure cessa, et redevint ce qu'il était, chancelant, la nuit divisée de ses ombres accomplies, la lueur qui s'était apparue dans son mirage dénué de cendres était la pure lumière et elle allait cette fois disparaître en le sein de l'ombre qui, ac-

> complie, revenue du corridor du temps, était
> enfin parfaite et éternelle, —elle-même, de-
> venue son propre sépulcre, dont les panneaux
> se retrouvaient ouverts sans bruit.

Here, Igitur is satisfied that he knows: no more doubt. The halt of his certitude was the same halt as the one in which the new polarity, *froissement*, appeared. He goes over all the phenomena: the heartbeat was the *scandement* and the light-dark rhythm of the shadow-file between the dark poles of the holes of past and future "nights"; all that is "finished" and "external," i.e., objective, understood. The *froissement* wasn't a bird but the velvet bust of an (this time, again, "superior") ancestral genius. The duality here (as in the old Midnight room) is again a shiver, which he understands as being only the foamy, wavy lace of his collar (like the wavy becoming of the spidery threads of doubt, previously). It is himself, that genius, objective in the night as appeared to self (symmetrically) in Igitur's neutral mind. At that, a unity appears in the cessation of (duality) sound, which becomes again *chancelant*,[2] i.e., no longer too-perfect but on the edge of falling into its "own tomb" (below). That understood and yet unconscious (*chancelant*) night vision with its shadow-file of understood shadows (*accomplies*) and the pure light of understanding, which is about to disappear in the *sein de l'ombre*; all that is really, "finally," perfect and eternal; that light (*elle*) has become its own tomb, as Igitur's idea cancels itself. The tomb is now open (that burial representing success) without noise, i.e., no more doubt or Becoming.

2. On Page 5 of the *Coup de Dés*—the Page of the *ombre puérile*, the son figure, who is akin to Hamlet and Igitur—his precarious hold on life is described as *chancelant*.

(Y)

Δ

L'ombre disparut dans les ténèbres futures,
y demeura avec une perception de balancier
expirant alors qu'il commence à avoir la sensation de lui: mais elle s'aperçut à l'étouffe-
ment expirant de ce qui luit encore dès qu'il
s'enfonce en elle—qu'elle rentre en soi, d'où
provenait par conséquent l'idée de ce bruit,
retombant maintenant en une seule fois inu-
tilement sur lui-même dans le passé.

Si d'un côté le doute disparaissait, scandé
nettement par le mouvement qui restait seul
du bruit, de l'autre la réminiscence du bruit
se manifestait par un vague frôlement inac-
coutumé, et cet état d'angoisse consciente
était comprimée vers le mirage par la per-
manence constatée des panneaux encore ouverts parallèlement et à la fois se fermant
sur eux, comme dans une spirale vertigineuse,
et à jamais fuyante si la compression prolongée n'eût dû impliquer la halte d'une expansion retenue, qui eut lieu en effet, et ne
fut troublée que par le semblant de volètement évasif d'un hôte de la nuit effrayé dans
son lourd sommeil, lequel disparut dans ce
lointain indéfini.

Here too there is little changed. The *ombre*, as before, is Igitur. The *ténèbres futures* are the stairwell
dark, which represents in advance the final dark of his
demise. The pendulum beat expires as it begins to have
a sensation of itself (*lui*); this is the "hesitation" of the
preceding passage, between pendulum and heart (a po-

larity at right angles to the pendulum beat as first polarity); the hesitation is also between the expiration of the
beat and its continuation—the heart seems to stop beating in its fright—but the shadow saw itself (*s'aperçut*)
in the movement of expiring or stifling of that which
shines (the consciousness) and which still shines as soon
as it sinks into it, the shadow. The shadow sees thus that
the sinking is its own, that it, the shadow, sinks back
into itself in that movement (the movement is the shadow's). That movement—Becoming—is now understood
to be the cause or "idea" (i.e., another obtrusive duality
is involved in "idea") of the bothersome noise, now understood or neutralized by the preceding dialectic, so
that it falls back on itself, canceled, into the past, useless
and harmless. The "doubt disappeared" (below).

Note that in the echo of *lui* and *luit* we have the paradoxical movement of expiration of light and continuation of it, one coming right out of the other (the *luit*
from the expired *lui*). This dialectic is also of the heart
hesitating and refinding life-beat from amidst its demise,
i.e., the supreme paradox of life from death, put in tetrapolar (and polypolar) terms—Igitur is down amid the
stuff of existence. In other words, if a heartbeat is a
positive-negative rhythm (diastole-systole more complexly) and we assimilate negation to a little death, the
hesitation between its stopping and starting again as a
whole (including the dual beat) is a tetrapolar extension
of this rhythm. And, as we implied, the rhythm of light-
dark in inner perception follows the same pattern. If
one looks inwardly at the rise and fall of the light of
consciousness, it is a familiar phenomenon that *right
within the contraction of the light to a nothing* in the
rising dark emerges the new light. And if we examine
this process, too, we can extend it to a vibrant (par-

adoxical) new dimension of itself, i.e., tetrapolar vibrancy.[3]

Si d'un côté: a duality still remains in the form of the canceled-out noise (a typical new start in the ever-renewed movement of life and thought); a dialectical synthesis always opens up again (through antisynthesis). The noise remains as movement, though the bothersome "idea" has retreated; the movement is of the disappearance itself, in any case, a meta-movement replacing the noise that has gone. On the other hand, the "reminiscence of the noise" is manifested by a brushing sound, as in previous passages: that is where the doubt re-emerges from amidst a symmetry-victory, which he tries to reestablish as before, this whirling struggle in him being the *angoisse consciente*. It becomes the familiar image of the open-closed panels, supreme whirling of infinite regress stopped by the flight of natural impulse, a "halt" in the *expansion retenue* (the antinomial struggle). The flight is assimilated to a bird as before; no new problem arises for us.

(Z)

La Nuit était bien en soi cette fois et sûre
que tout ce qui était étranger à elle n'était
que chimère. Elle se mira dans les panneaux
luisants de sa certitude, où nul soupçon n'eût
pu s'attacher de ses pattes arachnéennes, et si
jamais quelqu'hôte étranger à elle les avait
frôlés de ses plumes, c'étaient des génies
d'une espèce supérieure aux hôtes qu'elle
avait imaginés, pareille peut-être à celle de ses

---

3. René Daumal describes this kind of movement on the basis of his self-observation in semisuicidal experiments.

ombres apparues dans les panneaux, soucieux
de recueillir toute poussière d'elle pour que,
parvenue au point de jonction de son futur
et de son passé devenus identiques, elle se
mirât en toutes ces ombres apparues pures
avec le volume de leur destinée et la lueur
épurée de leur conscience. Tout était parfait,
en face et derrière ces deux épaisseurs ob-
scures identiques étaient bien les ténèbres
vécues par ces ombres revenues à leur état de
ténèbres, et divisées seulement à l'infini par
les marches faites des pierres funéraires de
toutes ces ombres. Toutes deux semblaient
identiquement pareilles, sauf que, de même
qu'elles étaient l'opposé des ombres, de même
elles devaient s'opposer l'une à l'autre, et,
les divisions tournant également sur elles-
mêmes, elles allaient différemment. Tout
était parfait; elle était la Nuit pure, et elle
entendit son propre cœur qui battit. Toute-
fois il lui donna une inquiétude, celle de trop
de certitude, celle d'une constatation trop
sûre d'elle-même: elle voulut se replonger à
son tour dans les ténèbres vers son sépulcre
unique et abjurer l'idée de sa forme telle
qu'elle s'était apparue par son souvenir des
génies supérieurs chargés de réunir ces cendres passées. Elle fut troublée un moment
par sa propre symétrie; mais, comprenant à
l'évasion trop grande de la clarté, atténuée
jadis, que cette évasion avait été le bruit de
l'oiseau dont le vol propagé lui avait semblé
continu, elle songea qu'en suivant cette lumière, lorsqu'elle recréerait un vertige pareil

au premier, elle retournerait à son évanouis-
sement. Elle reconnut en appliquant la lueur
devant les ténèbres laquelle des deux portes
il fallait prendre, à l'effet identique de la
lueur et, instruite maintenant de l'architecture des ténèbres, elle fut heureuse de per-
cevoir le même mouvement, et le même
froissement. Ce froissement était dans ce corridor où s'était enfui le bruit, pour disparaître
à jamais, non celui d'un hôte ailé de la nuit,
dont la lumière avait froissé le ventre velu,
mais le propre miroitement du velours sur le
buste d'un génie supérieur, et il n'y avait
d'autre toile arachnéenne que la dentelle sur
ce buste, et quant au mouvement qui avait
produit ce frôlement, c'était non la marche
circulaire d'une telle bête, mais la marche
régulière debout sur les deux pieds de la
race qui était apparue tenant dans deux mains
un volume et une lueur. Elle reconnaissait
son personnage ancien qui lui apparaissait
chaque nuit, mais enfin, maintenant qu'elle
l'avait réduit à l'état de ténèbres, après qu'il
lui fut apparu comme des ombres, elle était
libre enfin, sûre d'elle-même et débarrassée
de tout ce qui était étranger à elle. En effet,
le bruit cessa, en la lumière qui demeura seule
et pure.

Now, instead of merely a shadow "being in itself," it
is the "Night" as a whole that is the objective reality
made sure, authentic. All the rest is illusion, *chimère*; no
problem for Igitur. "*Elle*," the Night, is mirrored in

the shining walls of Her symmetrical certitude. No doubt can attach to those walls, spiderlike (all this is familiar by now), and if any guest stranger to the Night had brushed them with its feathers—a passing allusion to the bird, denied—it was genius of a superior sort to the ones it, the Night, had imagined. Here the Night is identified with Igitur making new discoveries. That species (*espèce*) was like, perhaps, that one (species) which had in the form of the shadow-file (*ses ombres*: the Night's) appeared in the shining walls—i.e., been made eternal through Igitur's perfect vision—those panels having been careful to collect all of Her dust (all imperfection) so that having arrived at the timeless juncture of past and future become identical—time stopped and reversible (as in Nietzsche)—She could mirror herself in all those shadows (in the file), appearing pure with the volume of their destiny (the *grimoire*) and the purified light of their consciousness. Nothing really new here.

All is perfect, ahead and behind (recalling the darker *trouées* at the ends of the corridor-stairwell): the two identical, obscure thicknesses (*ténèbres* is darker than *ombres*)[4] were the black shadows (authentic, deep) lived (as death-in-life) by the authentic *ombre* figures who had come back—in a death experience—to their black shadow state (*ténèbres*) and were thus made whole, except for the minimal becoming-division marked by the alternations of light in the form of their tombstones (a deathly, hence minimal and authentic, division by light) in the infinite series. The two thicknesses (*épaisseurs*) were identical (at the ends of the corridor), except that just as they were the opposite of

4. Mallarmé lamented that the dark word was made lighter by its bright é sound: "se fonce peu" ("Crise de vers," p. 364).

the shadows (shadows of shadows, i.e., even darker, "negative shadows," as they are called earlier, in fragment V), they must also be opposed to each other. Here, a difference between Becoming (the shadows in file, separated) and Being (the dark, deathly *ténèbres*) is naturally—*devaient* implies that naturalness—carried out in a division of the two death shadows (*ténèbres*), and both these divisions "turn on themselves, equally": the shadows in file *are* as well as *are not* the death-shadows; the two death-shadows *are* as well as *are not* the same. The *elles allaient différemment* is merely the same idea as the "opposition," now accounted for.

The next passage is unproblematic and repeats previous ones: the pure certitude is too perfect and meta-paradoxically asymmetric; *une constatation trop sûre d'elle-même*. So the Night wants to go back down into the *ténèbres* again and give up that "form." But it understands that the too-great light (once or "formerly" attenuated by a previous cancellation) is an evasion like a previously experienced one—the bird-flight that seemed continuous—and so if it follows the light, which would come to another symmetry of infinite regress, *vertige*, it would vanish again as before. In other words, by circling around to a previous symmetrical moment, whose asymmetrical evasion was a return of light (and flight), Igitur could overcome the problem of evasion.

Elle reconnut: applying the light of consciousness (in following the light in order to circle his way out of it) to the dark ends, he seeks in this idea of an asymmetric progress which end to take, which "door" of the corridor (formerly stairwell) to go through. He recognizes a symmetry by the identical effect of the light, which means that there is no way to take; this is confirmed by the fact that it is an *architecture des ténèbres* that the Night learns. Then it is "happy" to hear the same movement and brushing sound as before (i.e., its circling is working). It recalls that the brushing was in the corridor where the "noise" (doubt) had previously disappeared for good. Now again we see the old explanation: not a bird, but the genius with his velvet bust and the lace collar (and not the old spiderweb of doubt or suspicion), which produced by its shiver (*froissement*, cf. the shiver of the nearly fixed gleams in previous passages F and P), and it wasn't light shivering on a bird's hairy stomach, but, etc. And the movement that produced this brushing (*frôlement* this time)—Igitur gets at the underlying movement here—was that of his biped race: its regular walking replacing the heartbeat. The becoming-duality is accounted for in this acceptable way, shooing away the doubt-bird, which is rejected as a source of the progressive beat, since it, like many birds (feeding), walks in a circle. The ancestral walkers also have their familiar polarity-pair, the volume and candle. *Elle*, the Night, circling back successfully, recognized thus the old person who appeared "each night" (this is a new element, a look back at less-than-definitive premonitions of the final Midnight), but now that She had reduced that person (all those previous approximate imaginings of that person) into the state of *ténèbres* (deathly, definitive shadow)—after the person had appeared as a file of shadows (alternating with tombstones)—*Elle*, the night, was "free" and "pure." The doubt-noise stops, in the light that remained alone and pure: here the light is not bothersome anymore (though we know it will be).

(AA)

E

> L'ombre redevenue obscurité, la Nuit de-
> meura avec une perception douteuse de pen-
> dule qui va expirer en la perception de lui;
> mais à ce qui luit et va probablement s'étein-
> dre en soi, elle se voit encore qui le porte;
> c'est donc d'elle que venait le battement ouï,
> dont le bruit total tomba à jamais dans le
> passé (sur l'oubli).

The shadow disappears into obscurity as in previous variants—becomes it again, i.e., "gets out of its own way" by sinking out of consciousness, leaving only the pure, objective *Nuit*.

The same dialectic of duality doubled (at right angles) by its "doubtful" nature hesitates, as in previous passages, between being external or internal, etc. Its rise-and-fall dialectic, paradoxically vibrant—life from death—repeats what we have seen. Igitur thinks he recognized its nature, as being an integral part of the Night, the perfect totality; the "total noise"—the basic duality, or Becoming, that bothered his symmetry—was the "noise" of this *battement*, but it now falls harmlessly and permanently (*à jamais*) into its own kind of obscurity, the past (or *sur l'oubli*, falls into forgetfulness).

All this, too, is familiar by now.

(AB)

> D'un côté, si toute ambiguïté cessa, l'idée
> de motion dure de l'autre, régulièrement
> marquée par le double heurt impossible du
> pendule qui n'atteint plus que sa notion, mais

dont le frôlement actuel revient dans le possible, tel qu'il doit avoir lieu, pour combler l'intervalle, comme si tout le choc n'avait pas été la chute unique des portes du tombeau sur lui-même et sans retour; mais dans le doute né de la certitude même de leur perception, se présente une vision de panneaux à la fois ouverts et fermés, dans leur chute en suspens, comme si c'était soi qui, doué de leur mouvement, retournât sur soi-même en la spirale vertigineuse conséquente; qui devait être indéfiniment fuyante si une oppression progressive, poids de ce dont on ne se rendait pas compte, malgré que l'on se l'expliquait en somme, n'eût impliqué l'expansion certaine d'un intervalle futur, sa cessation, dans laquelle, lorsqu'elles se retrouvèrent, rien en effet ne s'entendit plus que le bruit d'un battement d'ailes effaré de quelqu'un de ses hôtes absurdes heurté dans son lourd somme par la clarté et prolongeant sa fuite indéfinie.

This is almost an exact duplicate of fragment H (Section II of the main text), second paragraph.

ambiguïté was *équivoque*: no important change here.

impossible: brings out merely the pendulum's hesitation between two positions, external, internal, etc.

plus que sa notion: the hesitation of the meaning of the beat, generally the same as in the main text, i.e., the beat fades as a sure identity into a mere notion and is replaced (at right angles), etc., etc.

expansion: replaces *évasion*, without important change.

elles se retrouvèrent: the *expansion* and *cessation*; they replace *se confondirent* and have the same sense of being canceled out by being (both) rediscovered, rather than confused into an obscure unity (together).

The rest is the same as in the main text.

(AC)

IV

MALGRÉ LA DÉFENSE DE SA MÈRE, ALLANT JOUER DANS LES TOMBEAUX

(*Interdiction de sa mère de descendre ainsi,— sa mère qui lui a dit ce qu'il avait à accomplir. Pour lui il va aussi dans un souvenir d'enfance, cette nuit recommandée s'il se tuait, il ne pourrait pas, grand, accomplir l'acte*).

Il peut avancer, parce qu'il va dans le mystère. (Ne descend-il pas à cheval sur la rampe toute l'obscurité, —tout ce qu'il ignore des siens, corridors oubliés depuis l'enfance.) Telle est la marche inverse de la *notion* dont il n'a pas connu l'ascension, étant, adolescent, arrivé à l'Absolu: spirale, au haut de laquelle il demeurait en Absolu, incapable de bouger, on éclaire et l'on plonge dans la nuit à mesure. Il croit traverser les destins de cette nuit fameuse: enfin il arrive où il doit arriver, et voit l'acte qui le sépare de la mort.

Autre gaminerie.

il boira exprès pour se retrouver

Il dit: je ne peux faire ceci sérieusement: mais le mal que je souffre est affreux, de vivre: au fond de cette confusion perverse et inconsciente des choses qui isole son absolu—il sent l'absence du moi, représentée par l'existence du Néant en substance, il faut que je meure, et comme cette fiole contient

le néant par ma race différé jusqu'à moi (ce
vieux calmant qu'elle n'a pas pris, les ancêtres
immémoriaux l'ayant gardé seul du naufrage), je ne veux pas connaître le Néant,
avant d'avoir rendu aux miens ce pourquoi ils
m'ont engendré—l'acte absurde qui atteste
l'inanité de leur folie. (L'inaccomplissement
me suivrait et entache seul momentanément
mon Absolu.)

The title is explained in the little marginal note, which
tells that Igitur's mother forbade his descent into the
tomb precisely so he wouldn't die as a child but would
live to accomplish the suicidal Act. This idea will be
developed in various sketches for the Great Work and,
especially, in the *Coup de Dés*: the *Fiançailles* (Page 5)
are a feminine principle of life that is on-going through
nonaccomplishment of the absolute, or the supreme
coup de dés. But little Igitur already has in germ his
fatal aim and plays in the tomb, as all children in a sense
do, approaching death in various ways. Under II (H)
I quoted a passage of Poe's *La Dormeuse*, in Mallarmé's
translation (p. 203); it describes a girl-child who threw
stones at the doors of her own future tomb, and, shivering with fear, listened to the dead groaning inside.

Il peut: the text here abandons the idea that Igitur
is still a child; only the memory of that puerile episode
in the tomb lingers. "He can advance because he goes
into mystery" means that this descent into the tomb is
not a sentimental evasive progress, a flight, but a deep
advance into death-mystery, so that he is justified.

(*Ne descend-il pas*: indeed he goes rapidly down—
very deeply, in the spirit of existential truth—as if in a
childish bannister slide, seeing all he had forgotten since

his early adventure into the tomb. (This implies that as a child he had come close to death, which is true in a sense. Children emerge from nothing and have fewer defenses against the awesome idea of death: "All children are mirrors of death," as Sartre said in *Les Mots*. One thinks of the future *Tombeau d'Anatole*.) The *corridors* are here confirmed to be the stairwell.

Telle est: the stairs go down to the ancestral tomb in the far past; the notion Igitur represents heroically ascended in the opposite direction from that past; he didn't know that ascent since he came to the notion as an adolescent discovering the absolute (in the "present"). The spiral may refer to the stairs (as one looks down on them, a spiral appearance), but mainly it refers to the gradual refinement of existence, through cycles, at the peak of which, as in the *Coup de Dés*, one has reached such an extreme of refinement that there is no more movement, no more room for sentimental or "human" action; the absurd truth takes over and is self-canceling, every light-phase of meaning is canceled immediately, ironically, by an absurd opposite, darkness. Igitur believes he is crossing through the destinies—the ancestral development leading to him—of that famous night, the Midnight of the Act. Finally he has come to the appointed place and time and sees the ultimate Act, which alone separates him from death.

Autre gaminerie: this relatively adult (or adolescent) Act will be another childish gesture like the one of Igitur's remembered childhood. Like Shakespeare in *Macbeth*, he thinks life is a "poor player," hence the *comédien* of fragment S.

Il dit: the absurd is not serious, by definition, and yet it is murderously so. To act absurdly is absurd, as Camus notes in *L'Homme révolté* (already in *Le Mythe de Sisyphe*, at the moment of suicide, he approaches this "tetrapolar" idea); but an absurd life, meaningless—"la farce à mener par tous" as Rimbaud put it in *Une Saison en enfer*—is torture. This complex moment of mediation of his tortured life[5] Igitur calls "cette confusion perverse et inconsciente des choses qui isole son absolu"; at the "bottom" of that mess is still the potential absence of himself in the substantive form of that drop of Nothing (poison). Igitur "must die." And that phial contains the Nothing put off until Igitur, the old *calmant* that the race didn't take, the immemorial ancestors having kept that alone from the shipwreck, i.e., the absolute (to be obtained through death) was avoided, put off by the whole living line. It, the absolute, is what was lost in the first shipwreck, the fall from the All, as on Pages 1 and 2 of the *Coup de Dés*. But Igitur won't die until he tells the ancestors why—his excuse for writing, that becoming-act, cf. Rimbaud's excuse for "detaching these few pages of a cursed man" at the outset of the *Saison en enfer* (an old writer's ploy justifying the impure act of writing). He'll tell them why they gave birth to him and thus to the final absurd act that attests the shallowness or hollowness of their sentimental lives; their *folie* was a belief in ordinary life and its meaning, as opposed to his *folie*, which denies theirs. If he didn't perform his Act he'd be haunted; even now its inaccomplishment—the Act is momentarily deferred as he relates—alone mars his absolute.

In the margin *il boira exprès pour se retrouver* implies that a Life will emerge from this death.

5. Cf. "le vieux mal de vivre" (*Pour un tombeau d'Anatole*, f. 168).

(AD)

Cela depuis qu'ils ont abordé ce château dans un naufrage sans doute—second naufrage de quelque haute visée.

Ne sifflez pas parce que j'ai dit l'inanité de votre folie! silence, pas de cette démence que vous voulez montrer exprès. Eh! bien il vous est si facile de retourner là-haut chercher le temps—et de devenir—est-ce que les portes sont fermées?

Moi seul—moi seul—je vais connaître le néant. Vous, vous revenez à votre amalgame.

Je profère la parole, pour la replonger dans son inanité.

Il jette les dés, le coup s'accomplit, douze, le temps (minuit)—qui créa se retrouve la matière, les blocs, les dés—

Alors (de l'Absolu son esprit se formant par le hasard absolu de ce fait) il dit à tout ce vacarme: certainement, il y a là un acte—c'est mon devoir de le proclamer: cette folie existe. Vous avez eu raison (bruit de folie) de la manifester: ne croyez pas que je vais vous replonger dans le néant.

Cela depuis: they first came to this château (which, as in the *Coup de Dés*, stands for the basic site of Man's Passion) in a shipwreck—a typical accident of life that brings men to their lands, as in ancient migrations chased by fate—reflecting the total "shipwreck" of the fall from All, as in the *Coup de Dés*. The *haute visée* is the *coup* itself that man eternally tries to pull off (as in *eritis sicut dii*) in order to equal God; again and again he fails, providentially—a happy fall (*felix culpa*)—thus creating existence. Mallarmé's account is parallel to the biblical Adamic way ending in redemption, Eden.

Ne sifflez pas: the theatrical moment, addressing the public of ancestors. The emptiness of their folly we have seen above, expressed here as the meaningless "sound and fury" of existence, the vain turmoil going nowhere (*démence*, cf. *dé* and *ultérieur démon immémorial* connected with *ancestralement* on Page 5 of the *Coup de Dés*). Igitur chides them and says it is easy to go back up to life and live chronological time (*temps*) and to become (*devenir*)—the doors of the tomb (or the stairs?) aren't closed, they are free to go up. "He alone will know the *Néant*. They will come back (always) to their 'amalgamations,' the promiscuous common lot."

He pronounces the word to replunge it into emptiness (silence, death); the word is self-canceling, absurd. He throws the dice, the throw is accomplished, twelve, the number of midnight (when the two hands become as one), the time that created (becoming) is ended, leaving only a nonflowing or nonbecoming matter, the (hard) blocks, the dice as pure objects uncontaminated by human purpose.

Then (his spirit forming itself from the absolute by the absolute chance of this fact, i.e., he has become, by his sacrificial acceptance of chance, a part of total chance, a part of All) he says to all the ancestral stir opposing him: "There is certainly an act here—it is my duty to proclaim it: this madness [mine, the absurd] exists." Hence he has saved the ancestral folly too: "You were right [noise of *folie*] to manifest it [the folly]: don't think I'll replunge you into the nothing." Here his own line is redeemed at the last, just as Mallarmé reconciled himself with the initially rejected public and the ancestors[6] in many of his later writings, such as *Conflit* and *Confrontation*, and in the whole stubbornly pursued notion of creating a new myth and rite for mankind in *Le Livre*.

6. Camus, in *Le Mythe de Sisyphe*, does the same with the nonabsurdists at the end of his introductory essay.

IV

Genesis

IN SEPTEMBER 1866, Villiers de l'Isle-Adam wrote to Mallarmé:

> Quand paraîtra le *Traité des pierres précieuses*? J'ai plus confiance en votre alchimie qu'en celle d'Auriol Théophraste Bombaste dit le divin Paracelse. Toutefois, je vous indiquerai les *Dogmes et Rituel de la haute magie* d'Eliphas Lévy. . . . Quant à Hegel, je suis vraiment heureux que vous ayez accordé quelque attention à ce miraculeux génie. . . .

The same month, Cazalis wrote to his friend: "Sois calme, comme un Hégelien, car tu es Hégelien, et c'est vraiment une religion que tu portes à ravir, l'Hégelianisme" (*Documents Mallarmé*, no. 6, 1977, p. 333).

The influence of Hegel on Mallarmé is still a controversial matter. Clearly, from the just-quoted letter, Mallarmé was aware of him. Villiers spoke of Hegel elsewhere as "le titan de l'esprit." Eugène Lefébure, another close friend, was called a "Hegelian" by Cazalis. Camille Mauclair, on the basis of conversations with the poet, claimed an important influence for the German philosopher. Sartre, in his "L'Engagement de Mallarmé" (*Obliques*, nos. 18–19, 1979, pp. 169–94), goes along with this view with little evidence except the triadic dialectic of Mallarmé's letter to Lefébure on Venus' classic beauty (thesis), Mona Lisa (antithesis), and finally his "Beauté critique" (synthesis). Mallarmé hardly needed Hegel for that.

On the other hand, Henri Charpentier, in an article published in the special Mallarmé number of *Les Lettres* (1948), noted that the copy of Hegel in Mallarmé's library, given to him by Villiers, seems not to have been read "either by the giver or the receiver." This has the ring of truth to it. Poets like Mallarmé don't read all that much and certainly not heavy philosophy like Hegel's. A letter, to Aubanel, of 23 August 1866 makes this point clearly: "Livres que je scrute et feuillette sans courage pour les terminer. Il est vrai que ce sont des livres de science et de philosophie, et que je veux *jouir* —par moi chaque nouvelle notion et non l'apprendre" (*Corr.*, p. 231). In his later correspondence, Mallarmé speaks similarly of the many books waiting to be read by his bed, which he cannot get to because of the urgency of his own work.

In an unpublished dissertation on Mallarmé and Yeats (Harvard, 1960), Paul de Man demonstrates through solid research that none of the important Hegelian texts that include the ideas closest to Mallarmé—such as the *Phenomenology of Mind*—were available to him at that time. Only the *Logic* and the *Philosophy of Nature* had been translated, and Mallarmé had very little German. One suspects that he looked at a few passages outlining general Hegelian principles, in a superficial article by Edmond Scherer published in the *Revue des deux mondes* (31 [15 February 1861]: 812–56), or perhaps Lefébure, during conversation in 1866 on the beach at Cannes—alluded to in a letter from that period—gave him some sketchy ideas about Hegel. Paul de Man—

convincingly to me—questions even this, after a close reading of Lefébure's correspondence.

There are only one or two terms in Mallarmé's theoretical *Notes*—jottings for a linguistic theory based on an epistemology characterized by paradox, "fiction"— that can be identified as clearly Hegelian:

> Le Verbe, à travers l'Idée et le Temps qui sont "la négation identique à l'essence" du Devenir devient le *Langage*. (p. 854)

The cited portion is the only undeniable connection with Hegel. The extreme paradox, which Mallarmé expresses in *Notes* as "la fiction . . . le procédé même de l'esprit" is indeed the core of Mallarmé's thinking, but is independent of Hegel: Mallarmé had formulated it long before in various letters from the crisis period, such as the "rien qui est la vérité, ces glorieux mensonges" (March 1866, to Cazalis). In the same letter he speaks of "le Néant, auquel je suis arrivé sans connaître le Bouddhisme," implying obviously that he owed it to no other source. Mallarmé's spontaneous ambivalence is recorded in his earliest poems, on the death of his sister or of Harriet Smyth, and is the very flavor of *Hérodiade* ("si la beauté n'était le mort," etc.). In sum, first, although one must grant an awareness of Hegel in Mallarmé's essential movement of mind, one is hardly justified in asserting more than that; second, I would claim, in agreement with Paul de Man, that Mallarmé did not really need Hegel, that he worked out the essential ideas in his own mind and that indeed they wouldn't have meant much to him if he hadn't. Moreover, already in *Igitur*, which embodies paradox epistemology very fully, Mallarmé has gone beyond, or bypassed, Hegel in his push beyond the triadic to the tetrapolar and polypolar universe of thought that is the great leap of the modern mind. The same is probably true of occult thought of the kind Villiers recommends to Mallarmé in the above-mentioned letter. Mallarmé takes pains, in the *Notes*, to keep his distance from the "pauvres kabbalistes" who commit the error, from a poet's viewpoint, of abstracting metaphors from the organic wholes that are the substance of art: "Détacher d'un Art des opérations qui lui sont intégrales et fondamentales pour les accomplir à tort, insolément, c'est encore une vénération, maladroite" (p. 850). A certain sympathy is expressed (contrasted with his scorn for the masses and fellow writers who malign both true poets and cabbalists), but with strong reservations.

Yet, as in the case of Hegel, if nothing can be asserted with absolute conviction in the way of influence, the parallels are interesting enough to be worthy of mention.

In the *Nuctemeron of Appolonius of Tyana*[1] published in the appendix to the *Dogme et rituel* of Lévi (Lévy, Villiers called him), we find a ritual in twelve phases corresponding to the twelve signs of the Zodiac (cf. *Notes*, p. 850: "lettres—spirituel zodiaque" in relation to the Kabbalah).

"Nuctéméron veut dire le jour de la nuit ou la nuit éclairée par le jour" (p. 364). This is parallel to the light-dark polarity and paradox of *Igitur*.

"Dans l'unité, les démons chantent les louanges de Dieu" (p. 365). The theme of unity is obviously important to our text, but not in these theological terms.

---

1. I pointed out the connection with this occult text in my earliest study of Mallarmé (*Mallarmé's Un Coup de Dés*, 1949) but, curiously, no one has followed up on it, so far as I know.

"Par le binaire . . . les serpents de feu s'enlacent autour du caducée et la foudre devient harmonieuse" (p. 365). The image of monsters or chimeras becoming fixed, in Igitur, is rather parallel.

"A la quatrième heure, l'âme retourne visiter les tombeaux, c'est le moment où s'allument les lampes magiques aux quartre coins des cercles, c'est l'heure des enchantements et des prestiges" (p. 365). This is very close: Igitur goes to the tombs in Section IV. The tetrapolar cross of his "perfect symmetry" is clearly echoed here (though, again, one cannot be sure of influence).

"L'âme des soleils correspond avec le soupir des fleurs, des chaînes d'harmonie font correspondre entre eux tous les êtres de la nature" (p. 366). Here we may think of the sky-sea reciprocity of Igitur. There are fascinating echoes in Baudelaire's *Correspondances*, *Elevation* (sky-flowers), Rimbaud's *Phrases* ("guirlandes d'étoile en étoile") . . .

"Les ailes des génies s'agitent avec un bruissement mystérieux" (p. 367). One thinks of the *génies* with their feather dusters and their *frôlement* and other such mysterious whisperings in *Igitur*.

"Génies de la quatrième heure . . . génie du jeu" (p. 369). This idea of *jeu* is important to the *Igitur* text and to Mallarmé's central evolution.

"Il triomphe ainsi de la fatalité qui est le génie du jeu" (p. 369). This was at times the (vain) hope of Igitur.

"La *quintessence* . . . harmonie qui résulte de l'analogie et du *mariage des contraires*" (p. 370). Clear echo of moments of our text.

Passing now to a Hebraic version of the *Nuctemeron*:

"L'homme est la synthèse du monde créé, en lui recommence l'unité créatrice. . . ." (p. 375). Igitur's ambition is reflected here, as is the all-seeking *coup* of the *Coup de dés*.

"Toute force et toute vie résulte de deux" (p. 375). The basic polarity of *Igitur*.

"L'organe générateur qui est composé d'un et de deux, figure du nombre ternaire" (p. 375). The phallic overtones in *Igitur* have been noted in our commentary.

"Le ternaire sort de lui-même du binaire" (p. 375). This happens in our text, setting up the need for the next stage.

"Le quaternaire qui donne en géométrie la croix et le carré qui est le nombre parfait" (p. 376). Clearly parallel to the core passages of Igitur's "symmétrie parfaite."

"Douzième heure. . . . L'homme et la femme subissent leur peine, l'expiation commence et le libérateur est promis" (p. 378). This twelfth hour end-of-cycle (and beginning of another) sacrificial moment (death-Life) is the essence of *Igitur*, from the initial *Minuit*, which reflects the paradoxical beginning-end, to the final *coup* "douze" of that *Minuit* rebegun in the last section. In a previous passage (p. 373) we read: "Il faut savoir se sacrifier pour renaître immortel."

In the foregoing pages, I have emphasized my belief that anyone going down deeply enough will encounter the archetypical patterns common to mankind in all ages and that on these grounds we ought not to speak of influence but rather of Kierkegaardian "repetitions" of the old truths.[2]

In terms of traditional parallels, Bettina Knapp's fine article, "Igitur or Elbehnon's Folly" (*Yale French Studies*, no. 54, 1977), offers some interesting further examples. None of them, however, can be persuasively said to have been known to Mallarmé and none come quite as close to his text as the cited passages of Eliphas Lévi.

Not entirely convincing but closer are some examples presented by Kurt Wais in an article, "Igitur Mallarmés" (*Comparative Literature Studies* 4, nos. 1 and 2 [1967]): he detects a general source of dark atmosphere in Charles Maturin's *Melmoth the Wanderer*, various tales of Poe, and Baudelaire's *La Chambre double* (I don't see this example at all); the Piranesi-like spiral stair had predecessors in Coleridge, Thomas De Quincey, and Alfred de Musset. Especially interesting is a passage from Théophile Gautier's *Club des hashischins*: "L'escalier ... prenait à travers mon rêve des proportions cyclopéennes et gigantesques. Ses deux bouts noyés d'ombre me semblaient plonger dans le ciel et dans l'enfer." Or this from Musset's *Confessions d'un enfant du siècle*: "Il semble que l'homme soit vide, et

2. I don't hold, however, with Noam Chomsky's view of built-in patterns of language, for example. Language is dialectically both inner (never simply "inborn") and outer, beyond any hypothetical horizontal line of passive or neutral human awareness at a given time, and this is its creative freedom *ab origine*. This dialectic is a version of Mallarmé's "fiction" at the heart of his linguistic fragments (*Notes*). Jung's archetypes have been subjected to Lacanian critique on the same grounds. For operative (scientific or logical) purposes, the theories of Jung and Chomsky hold true enough to be useful, although they are not very profound. At the end of his life, Jung acknowledged the problem to his disciple Maria Fremd.

MALLARMÉ: *IGITUR*

qu'à force de descendre en lui il arrive à la dernière marche d'une spirale. Là, comme au . . . fond des mines, l'air manque et Dieu défend d'aller plus loin." Finally, there is a section of the *Légende des siècles* of Hugo entitled *Eviradnus* that contains a few suggestive echoes. An underground burial chamber, with spiderwebs and a double file of dead warriors on their horses, a "confrontation de fantômes dans l'ombre" that Wais sees as parallel to the row of spectres in *Igitur*. Outside of the Musset piece, none of this is very secure.

In chapter 1, I stated my reasons for not accepting the thesis of Roland de Renéville concerning the origin of the name *Igitur* in the Vulgate and offered instead what I considered to be likelier sources, in Beckford and Villiers, etc. I will not go over that ground again here, other than to say that the Hamlet figure inherited directly from Shakespeare joins with the spiritually virile, passionately lucid apparition of Descartes; with the juvenile author of Vathek as Mallarmé describes him in his elegant preface and as Byron alludes to him in verses from *Childe Harold* quoted by Mallarmé; with Villiers himself merged with the youthful, somewhat androgynous, heroine of *Isis*; with the stripling Musset as we glimpse him in the *Confessions*; with the aristocratic young Vigny; with Balzac's Louis Lambert (suggested by A. Orliac); with a flash of Keats and Chatterton; with Roderick Usher; and so on, all together forming something like the series of ancestral phantoms leading to Igitur himself in the stairway and corridor leading to eternity.

Starting with the fountainhead in this series, Shakespeare, what is left of the "juvénile fantôme, ombre de nous tous"? The solitary communion with death, the past (including an ocean voyage and a hint of cosmic shipwreck), the dead ancestor, and the suicidal mood and *folie* throughout; the eerie whispered "list, list" of the ghost from the past; an infantile relation to the mother; an actual leaping into the grave, in one scene; the topos of the book as the world, to be extinguished together. There is a sense of the prolixity of the past—"words words words words words" and the "fond trivial records"—as compared with the laconic single deed of self-annihilation. At this juncture we catch a wisp of *Macbeth* (exegetized by Mallarmé) and its theme of the blown-out candle, self-destruction, faced with the "sound and fury," the folly of absurd existence. In the naked and gloomy royal site of Elseneur we detected a possible echo of Elbehnon, together with other putative source-echoes, outlined in chapter 1; nothing comes any closer to *Igitur*, subsequently, than all of this . . .

Passing to Poe, the central atmosphere of a late heir of an aristocratic line in a lugubrious and claustral manorial setting is found not only in *The Fall of the House of Usher*, which Mallarmé declared to be a favorite of his, but in various other tales of Poe as well. For example, there is *Berenice*: the hero's name *Egaeus* may be a part of the cluster of echoes in Igitur that we treated in chapter 1 (as may be *Ligeia*, from another tale). In the "Homme-Dieu" chapter of *Les Paradis artificiels*, Baudelaire refers to this "metaphysician" and his penchant for "forgetting himself through a whole night watching the narrow flame of a light" or "repeating in a monotonous manner some vulgar word until by dint of repetition the sound ceased presenting any idea to the mind."[3] These themes are close indeed to our text.

3. Baudelaire, *Oeuvres complètes*, Gallimard, 1958, p. 463. My translation.

As for the setting, we find this: "Our line has been called a race of visionaries . . . the family mansion . . . [had a] library chamber. In that chamber was I born . . . addicted to the most intense and painful meditation."[4] In *Ligeia*, the Germanic tone we found in Elbehnon is in "some large old decaying city near the Rhine" (p. 324). A similar tone is in the title place of *The Domain of Arnheim*, which is not located but is compared to Beckford's Fonthill. That never-never Germany of the Romantics, which came down into the French tradition, as Albert Béguin relates it, through the nineteenth century and beyond, was as attractive to Poe's transcendental temperament at it would be to the Symbolists he influenced.

Another mysterious setting is in *Shadow, a Parable*:

> at night. . . . to our chamber there was no entrance save by a lofty door of brass . . . fastened from within. Black draperies, likewise, in the gloomy room, shut out from our view the moon. . . . a sense of suffocation—anxiety. . . . A dead weight. . . . upon the household furniture. . . . in the mirror . . . each of us . . . beheld the pallor of his own countenance. . . . young Zoilus. Dead . . . the genius and the demon of the scene. (Pp. 269–70)

Although there is much here that we find in the imagery of *Igitur*, I include this only suggestively. One assumes that Mallarmé read it, committed as he was to Poe.

Returning to *Usher*: "A small picture presented the interior of an immensely long and rectangular vault or tunnel, with low walls, smooth, white and without interruption or device . . . at an exceeding depth below the surface of the earth" (p. 279). There are other such

4. *The Best Known Works of Edgar A. Poe*, Blue Ribbon Books, 1927, p. 313. Subsequent references to Poe will be indicated by page numbers alone.

underground chambers in *The Cask of Amontillado*, *The Pit and the Pendulum*, etc. In the poem, *The Sleeper*, there is:

> Some vault that oft hath flung its black
> And winged panels fluttering back,
>
> .   .   .   .
>
> Some sepulchre, remote, alone,
> Against whose portals she hath thrown,
> In childhood many an idle stone—
>
> .   .   .   .
>
> It was the dead who groaned within.

Here, as we noted earlier, there are touches of the child playing about a tomb in *Igitur*, the twin panels and the wing-bird image that arises therefrom as well as from the night, and some spooky sounds, corresponding to the whispering in the stairway leading to the grave.

The fact that Roderick Usher was "the last of an ancient race" and that "the entire family lay in the direct line of descent" gives him a sort of fine-spun, in-bred delicacy (one thinks of the single file of phantoms in *Igitur*, leading to the final Hamlet figure), so that he had "hair of more than web-like softness and tenuity." The spidery ruff on Igitur's velvet costume and the image of his hair in the midnight mirror of horror seem related to this atmosphere; perhaps the other "arachnean" imagery is related, as well.

Finally, there is in the *Colloquy of Monos and Una* a death and rebirth theme—as so often in Poe—leading to a concept of "duration," an essence of pure temporality and spatiality, almost like Kantian categories of time and space, which are at least in the same direction as Igitur's apocalyptic and eschatological meditations. The *lieu* of the *Coup de Dés*, after the departure of man, is equally empty, "rien n'aura eu lieu que le lieu"; likewise time, in its essential form, is echoed in various terms of the final page vibrating in absurd antinomies.

Above all, in Poe there is the model of *The Raven*: the midnight vigil of the mind, the night-spawned bird, the claustral setting of the room, the uneasy curtains, the theme of death and the death of sentimental hope: "Nevermore."

In the small library at Valvins, there is a copy of Vigny's poetry that Mallarmé owned as a young student. Certainly Vigny is, as Jean Moréas opined in his famous manifesto, among the great precursors of Symbolism in general (as well as of Proust in particular). Mallarmé was clearly taken with *La Bouteille à la mer*, which was very much on his mind when he composed his *Coup de Dés*. The imagery of poetry as the great new heroic feat of mankind, as a hard diamond crystallizing and condensing reality into something that outlives cities, won ready sympathy from young Mallarmé.

In earlier pages we have shown the important influence of *L'Esprit pur* on the imagery of *Igitur*. Here, I will merely repeat the key strophe:

> Dans le caveau des miens plongeant mes
>   pas nocturnes,
> J'ai compté mes aïeux, suivant leur
>   vieille loi.
> J'ouvris leurs parchemins, je fouillai
>   dans leurs urnes
>
> .   .   .   .
>
> A peine une étincelle a relui dans leur
>   cendre.
> C'est en vain que d'eux tous le sang m'a
>   fait descendre;
> Si j'écris leur histoire, ils descendront
>   de moi.

This proud boast of a delicate intellectual heir finds an obvious echo in Igitur's aim to rescue his ancestral line from their failure to conquer fate, or chance, by a psychically suicidal sacrifice. Indeed, this is Vigny's constant message: that only now, in the fullness of time, as in the spirit of Hegel's *Phenomenology of Mind*, can a supreme heroic thinker arise to justify mankind. This sacrificial note—echoed also in *Prose* (*pour des Esseintes*)—is expressed in *La Bouteille à la mer*: "Sur la pierre des morts croît l'arbre de grandeur." The notion of a spiritual seed descending on the modern brow is in the last strophe:

> Le vrai Dieu, le Dieu fort, est le Dieu
>   des idées.
> Sur nos fronts où le germe est jeté par
>   le sort,
> Répandons le Savoir en fécondes ondées;
> . . . .
> Jetons l'oeuvre à la mer, la mer des
>   multitudes. . . .

This aristocratic yet caring attitude, heroic and almost jaunty in its courage despite the vast odds it lucidly contemplates in Man's war against a capricious fate, is present in poems like *Salut*, *Au seul souci*, *A la nue*, and the *Coup de Dés* itself, and some of it marks the solitary daring of young Igitur as well.

Mallarmé could have gotten this message from Vigny's prose as well: *Le Poète et la vie*, *Le Journal du poète*, etc. There too he could have learned that "l'espérance est la plus grande des folies" and found references to suicide and the dice game of fate. But none of this, of course, is decisive.

Far more convincing is the example of Baudelaire,

particularly *L'Horloge*, as we treated it in chapter 1. The whole Baudelaire atmosphere of struggle with absurd fate, in the agonized lineage of Hamlet, the stark imagery that arises therefrom in black and white tones and grotesque Piranesi-like spirals or other pure geometric lines emerging from sheer spiritual wrestling, all this is most germane to *Igitur*, as it is to Mallarmé altogether. Baudelaire's essay on Hugo is especially important in this respect, as I have shown in my studies of the *Coup de Dés*. Hugo himself, of course, is a part of this "underground" lineage, at times anticipatory of surrealism, as we noted earlier. But this is extremely general and suggestive, too vague to indicate direct influence.

Indeed, the more one looks at the question, the more one is struck by the remarkable originality of *Igitur*. What a leap of intellect and vision it is, after all!

Previous Studies

THE ESSENTIAL DRAMA of *Igitur* is presented, very approximately, by Jean-Pierre Richard in his *Univers imaginaire de Mallarmé*, although we have to dismiss his suggestion that *Elbehnon* may refer to "El be none . . . , le 'ne sois personne' " as far-fetched. Richard tries to put the complex dialectic that is the core of *Igitur* in terms of a combination of "zigzag" and "spiral." These terms are adequate but unwieldy and are not susceptible to extension to the entire work, where in truth they are omnipresent in the flexible form of polypolarity. Moreover, Richard, as Genette and Derrida have noted in well-known critiques, short-circuits his dialectic, finding a sort of success in the maneuver comparable to the synthetic *bonheur* he finds throughout Mallarmé's *oeuvre*.

Richard devotes only two or three pages to a given important work and ties its imagery to that of many other works, as in his commentary on the diamond, which for him is a crystallization of *néant*, a vibrant nothing-essence. *D'accord*, that is indeed Mallarmé's essential strategy, an objectification through *néantisation* of something as beautiful and enduring as the distant stars, and indeed that is the way his most characteristic images function: they are mediators of the

Nothing-All. But Richard's kind of analysis becomes repetitious and sprawling, and it does not respect the integrity of each work or the true integrity of the Vision. It seems preferable not to use works thus to illustrate a scientific hypothesis showing just a facet or two that join to a network of theory, but to respect the full complexity of each work. One should only incidentally draw on other examples—no more than absolutely necessary for the poem in question—to pin down critical points, moving in this way gradually, naturally, toward a total perspective. There is room, to be sure, for prefatory or epilogual critical synthesis, when more is needed in the way of intertextuality, but that enterprise demands something rather chosen and compact in order to be Mallarméan.

René Nelli's brief article *"Igitur" ou l'argument ontologique retourné* understands the basic drama too and puts it rather well, but dismisses the whole affair too quickly. Nothing in the article shows any awareness of the new kind of dialectic at work there; nor, in its limited scope, does it go very far in exploring the imagery or other critical issues.

In a few choice pages (197–203) of *La Révolution du langage poétique*, Julia Kristeva sketches some important themes of *Igitur*: the espousal of *folie* and chance in revolt against a bourgeois order; the perverse movement toward the mother in a parallel dialectic. She observes the phallic nature of the unicorn's horn (though I do not see the *corps né* in *cornet*). Brief as her study is, it is impressively intelligent work. Admittedly building on Kristeva's work, Jean-Luc Steinmetz, in an article "Mallarmé en corps" (*Littérature*, no. 17, 1975, pp. 105–28), repeats the essential notions but moves very quickly on to other matters in his romp through the complete works of the master in twenty-three pages.

As much as one admires the ambition and mental dexterity of the *Tel Quellistes*, including Pierre Rottenberg (treated in chapter 1) and Jean-Luc Steinmetz, there are some strong reservations to be stated generally about the movement: burdened with semiotic apparatus and jargon, and blinkered by the Marxist-materialist view—which does less than full justice to Mallarmé's rounded "aesthetic" universe, much as was the case with Charles Mauron's psychological approach[1]—they tend to get out of Mallarmé what they put in. The semiotic dialectic, despite some advances beyond Hegel in Derrida and Kristeva (the "fourth term"), does not attain the suppleness of Mallarmé's epistemology, at one pole, while at the pole of artistic presence, the concrete work of the language through sound and imagery and the overall "Jeu suprême," the approach is skimpy.

A recently published book by Rolf Stabel, *"Igitur," Mallarmé's Erfahrung der Literatur*, has come belatedly to my attention. It was a doctoral dissertation at Freiburg and is quite thorough. But Stabel too misses the fundamental Mallarméan dialectic: for example, he sees the opening and shut tomb panels as a beat representing *linear* time, punctuated by sounds of the clock or strokes of the pendulum. One can hardly understand why this standard series would entail such complex and mysterious symbolism and maneuvering of the mind. Stabel falls for the Jesuitic tactic in Paul Claudel's "Catastrophe d'Igitur": Claudel hypocritically praises *Igitur* in order to pull down with it the whole non-Catholic nineteenth century. He sees it as the essential drama of the claustral God-refusing soul in his time, hiding in a gloomy mid-

1. See my article "Mauron on Mallarmé," *Modern Language Notes* 78, no. 5 (Dec. 1963): 520–26.

night room from the glorious cosmos that proclaims the Creation. This has nothing to do with Mallarmé, of course, who took on, as it were, all outdoors and "magnified" it as much as other non-Catholic sister-souls such as Debussy or Pissarro. Call them pantheist if you like, or something more elusively believing, *n'importe*. But I fail to see why one would feel closer to Eden listening to Mallarmé's or Debussy's *Faune* by imagining the creature with a crucifix dangling from his neck.

It is hard to understand why Stabel lists neither my compact but thorough outline of the meaning of *Igitur* (presented as an appendix to my *Oeuvre de Mallarmé: Un Coup de Dés* in 1951), nor my article "Wherefore Igitur?" (*Romanic Review*, no. 60, 1969) in his fairly lengthy bibliography. The appendix precedes by a year what Stabel sees as the first serious work on the text (Kurt Wais, *Mallarmé*, 1952) and also precedes most of the other items in his bibliography. I have not made much use of recent secondary literature here, in fact, because the meaning of the hermetic text came to me in the original insights that opened Mallarmé's universe to me thirty some years ago.

Bibliography

I. Works by Mallarmé

Oeuvres complètes. Edited by H. Mondor and G. Jean-Aubry. Bibliothèque de la Pléiade, 1945.

Igitur ou la folie d'Elbehnon. Edited by E. Bonniot. Gallimard, 1925.

"Igitur, fragment inédit" ("Longtemps, oh! longtemps..."). Edited by H. Charpentier. In *Les Lettres* 3 (1948): 24.

Igitur, Divagations, Un Coup de Dés. Preface by Yves Bonnefoy. Gallimard, 1976.

Mallarmé lycéen. Edited by H. Mondor. Gallimard, 1954.

Le "Livre." Edited by J. Schérer. Gallimard, 1957.

Les Noces d'Hérodiade: Mystère. Edited by G. Davies. Gallimard, 1959.

Pour un "Tombeau d'Anatole." Edited by J.-P. Richard. Seuil, 1961.

Stéphane Mallarmé: Correspondance, 1862–1871. Edited by H. Mondor. Gallimard, 1959.

Documents Mallarmé. No. 6. Edited by Carl P. Barbier. Nizet, 1977.

II. Books and Articles on Mallarmé

Austin, L. J. *Mallarmé et le rêve du "Livre."* Mercure de France, 1953.

Blanchot, M. *Faux pas.* Gallimard, 1943.

———. *La Part du feu.* Gallimard, 1949.

———. *L'Espace littéraire.* Gallimard, 1955.

———. *Le Livre à venir.* Gallimard, 1959.

———. *L'Entretien infini.* Gallimard, 1969.

Bolle, Louis. "Mallarmé, Igitur et Hamlet." *Critique* 21 (1965): 853–63.

Claudel, P. "La Catastrophe d'Igitur." *Nouvelle Revue française,* 1 November 1926, p. 531.

Cohn, Robert Greer. *Mallarmé's Un Coup de Dés.* A Yale French Studies Publication. Yale French Studies, 1949.

———. *L'Oeuvre de Mallarmé: Un Coup de Dés.* Librairie Les Lettres, 1951.

———. *Toward the Poems of Mallarmé.* University of California Press, 1965.

——— *Mallarmé's Masterwork: New Findings,* Mouton, 1966.

———. "Wherefore Igitur?" *Romanic Review* 60 (1969): 174–77.

———. "Mallarmé's Windows." *Yale French Studies,* no. 54, 1977, pp. 23–31.

———. "The Mallarmé Century." *Stanford French Review* 2, no. 3 (Winter 1978): 431–49.

———. "Mallarmé contre Genette." *Tel Quel,* no. 69, Spring 1977, pp. 51–54.

Cooperman, H. *The Aesthetics of Stéphane Mallarmé.* Koffern Press, 1933.

Ghil, René. *Les Dates et les oeuvres.* Crès, 1923.

Knapp, Bettina. "Igitur . . ." *Yale French Studies,* no. 54, 1977, pp. 188–213.

Kristeva, Julia. *La Révolution du langage poétique.* Seuil, 1974.

Les Lettres 3, 1948 (special number on Mallarmé).

Michaud, Guy. *Mallarmé.* Hatier-Boivin, 1952.

Mondor, H. *Vie de Mallarmé.* Gallimard, 1946.

Moore, G. *Avowals.* Heinemann, 1936.

Nelli, R. " 'Igitur' ou l'argument ontologique retourné." *Les Lettres* 3 (1948): 147–54.

Poulet, G. *Études sur le temps humain*:

    I. *Études sur le temps humain.* Plon, 1950.

    II. *La Distance intérieure.* Plon, 1952.

de Renéville, R. *L'Expérience poétique*. A la Baconnière, 1938.

Richard, J.-P. *L'Univers imaginaire de Stéphane Mallarmé*. Seuil, 1961.

Rottenberg, Pierre. "Une Lecture d'*Igitur*." *Tel Quel* no. 37 (1967): 74–94.

Sollers, Philippe. "Littérature et totalité." *Tel Quel* no. 26 (1966): 81–95.

Stabel, Rolf. *Igitur*. Fink, 1976.

Steinmetz, Jean-Luc. "Mallarmé en corps." *Littérature* no. 17 (1975): 105–28.

Wais, K. *Mallarmé: Dichtung, Weisheit, Haltung*. Beck, 1952.

———. "Igitur Mallarmés." *Comparative Literature Studies* 4, nos. 1 and 2 (1967): 35–43.

III. Other Books

Cohn, Robert Greer. *The Writer's Way in France*. University of Pennsylvania Press, 1960.

———. *Modes of Art*. Anma Libri, 1975.

Lévi, Eliphas. *Dogme et rituel de la haute magie*. Editions Niclaus, 1960.

Poe, Edgar Allan. *Best Known Works of Edgar A. Poe*. Blue Ribbon Books, 1927.

Designer: Wolfgang Lederer
Compositor: Heritage Printers
Printer: Heritage Printers
Binder: The Delmar Company
Text: Janson Linotype
Display: Janson